NEW MARKETS,
NEW STRATEGIES

NEW
MARKETS,
NEW
STRATEGIES

*Wealth-Building Habits for
Intelligent Investing*

Jason Trennert

MCGRAW-HILL

*New York   Chicago   San Francisco   Lisbon   London   Madrid
Mexico City   Milan   New Delhi   San Juan   Seoul
Singapore   Sydney   Toronto*

1 2 3 4 5 6 7 8 9 0   DOC/DOC   0 9 8 7 6 5 4

ISBN 0-07-144060-7

McGraw-Hill books are available at special discounts to use as premiums and sales promotions, or for use in corporate training programs. For more information, please write to the Director of Special Sales, McGraw-Hill Professional, Two Penn Plaza, New York, NY 10121-2298. Or contact your local bookstore.

This publication is designed to provide accurate and authoritative information in regard to the subject matter covered. It is sold with the understanding that the publisher is not engaged in rendering legal, accounting, or other professional service. If legal advice or other expert assistance is required, the services of a competent professional person should be sought.
> —*From a Declaration of Principles jointly adopted by a Committee of the American Bar Association and a Committee of Publishers and Associations*

 This book is printed on recycled, acid-free paper containing a minimum of 50% recycled de-inked paper.

Library of Congress Cataloging-in-Publication Data
Trennert, Jason.
  New markets, new strategies : wealth-building habits for intelligent investing / by Jason Trennert.
    p. cm.
  Includes index.
  ISBN 0-07-144060-7 (hardcover : alk. paper)
  1. Investments. 2. Portfolio management. 3. Investments—United States. 4. Portfolio management—United States. I. Title.
  HG4515.T74 2004
  332.6—dc22

                                                                                      2004010481

Alla famiglia

ACKNOWLEDGMENTS

PRESIDENT KENNEDY ONCE QUIPPED after the Bay of Pigs, "Success has many fathers, but failure is an orphan." I don't yet know whether the many people who helped to make *New Markets, New Strategies* possible will wish to take some small credit for it or would rather that I forgot their involvement in the project altogether. I do know, however, that regardless of what the critics may say, I will be forever grateful for the time, aid, and patience of a great many individuals extended to me during the sometimes arduous process of writing a book.

First and foremost, I'd like to thank my editor, Kelli Christiansen, for originally conceiving of the idea for this book and for putting up with the anxieties of a first-time author.

It goes without saying that *New Markets, New Strategies*—and my entire career, for that matter—would not have been possible without the gigantic leaps of faith and misplaced confidences exhibited by the partners of my firm, Ed Hyman, Nancy Lazar, and Jim Moltz of International Strategy & Investment. It may be hard to believe, but Ed Hyman, despite the fact that he has been ranked the number one economist on Wall Street in each of the last 24 years by *Institutional Investor*, may be an even better businessman than he is an economist; Nancy Lazar works harder than anyone I've seen in our business, which is remarkable; and Jim Moltz exudes a level of erudition and class one sadly only sees these days in black-and-white motion pictures. I have learned a great deal from them all as students of the financial markets and as human beings.

My right-hand man at ISI, Nick Bohnsack, may know more about the stock market than any other 25-year-old in the country and is responsible for many of the charts and more than a few insights in the pages that follow. (For the purposes of full disclosure, in the new regulatory environment on the Street, I bought him a humidor to at least partially compensate him for his efforts.)

Of course, I have benefited greatly from my association with CNBC, and I would be remiss if I didn't thank the friends and associates I have developed at the network through the years. Consuelo Mack is a consummate professional whose experience and lack of pretension make her one of the classiest people in business news. Her constant encouragement and guidance helped shape the final draft. Larry Kudlow and Jim Cramer have also been kind enough to have me on their hit eponymous show from time to time. Both stars in the investment business, I continue to learn a great deal from their unique insights on the current issues affecting business and the financial markets. Larry was particularly helpful and influential on the chapters dealing with dividends and the growing importance of Washington in the inner workings of the financial markets. A good man and a man of faith, Larry has also become a great mentor and friend. I also need to thank a fellow paisan and a heavy hitter in the world of business news, Ron Insana. From our meeting to discuss this project at the Tenafly Diner through his help in editing the final product, I will never forget Ron's generosity with his time and insight. Finally, thanks to Mark Harris and the guys on *Squawk Box* for having me on their show from time to time.

I benefited greatly from the suggestions in terms of style and content of Mike Santoli of Barron's, one of the most talented scribes on the financial markets in the country.

Robert McMahon, Bob Sherman, and Gavin Anderson of GovernanceMetrics helped me a great deal with the chapter on corporate governance. Thanks also to Joe Gatto of Starmine for his help with the chapter on sell-side research. All of these men are trailblazers of today's new Wall Street.

And then there are my firm's clients, without whose support I would have trouble feeding my family. Bill Chandler of Invesco, Mike Mach of Eaton Vance, and Steve Neimeth of Sun America were all extremely helpful in the development of the Thrifty Fifty concept. All great customers, they have become valued friends and advisers as well. In the purposes of full disclosure, Bill actually coined the term "Thrifty Fifty," forever saving me from having to write and speak about the "Sporty Forty." I am also extremely thankful for the advice and consent of Lee Cooperman and Steve Einhorn of Omega Advisors. Both former titans in the world of portfolio strategy, their work at Goldman Sachs was the foundation upon which my Market Balance Sheet is based.

Bob Froehlich of Deutsche Bank; Brian Wesbury of Griffin, Kubick, Stevens, and Thompson; Dean Dordevic of Ferguson Wellman; and my best friend in life, Jay Coyle of Frontpoint Partners—all urged me to take on the challenge that this book represented, and for that I am thankful. My buddy, broker, lawyer, and confidante, Steve Hadley, was extremely helpful in the initial and final stages of the project.

Of course, it is dangerous to write such lists for fear of leaving someone out, but I also owe a debt of gratitude to Larry Auriana of the Federated Kauffman Funds and Frank Felicelli of Franklin Templeton for their roles as friends and advisers. Legendary investor and consummate Southern gentleman, Julian Robertson, was generous with his time and was more than patient in explaining to me some of the finer points of the hedge fund business.

Finally, I need to thank the good Lord for my family's encouragement.

It might seem odd for a 36-year-old man to admit that his parents still check his homework, but a special thanks needs to be paid to my mom and dad for their constant encouragement and help during the final editing process. I am very thankful for many things my parents have given me, but I am most thankful to them for instilling in me a respect for learning. Both former public high school English teachers, their countless reviews of the manuscript made the final product tighter and more readable. Like all children, I didn't always listen to their suggestions, so any grammatical or syntax errors that remain are entirely my own. Semper Fi.

Finally, my lovely wife Bev has always been my biggest cheerleader through thick and thin, and my son Dominic has a truly remarkable ability to brighten any day. They were both constant sources of inspiration for every word on every page.

CONTENTS

Part II

A FRAMEWORK FOR INVESTING

INTRODUCTION

IN ALL THE YEARS I lobbied my boss and legendary Wall Street economist Ed Hyman for the job, I never imagined how lonely, frightening, and demoralizing it could be as a Wall Street strategist in the midst of a bear market. Of course, dramatic events in our professional lives are made all the more vivid by drama in our personal lives, and the dreamlike quality of seeing a quote screen filled with red numbers was only heightened by the birth of my son Dominic in July 2002.

Being of Italian descent, I know of few things that can compete in importance with the birth of any child, especially a boy. But as much as I hate to admit it, I was so worried about the burgeoning scandals in corporate America and its concomitant impact on stock prices that I made sure my assistant provided me with updates on the Dow and the Nasdaq every half hour while I was in the delivery room. Fortunately, my wife had long since become accustomed to such incursions into our private lives, but in retrospect the conclusion was clear—the market's decline was serious, scary, and unusual.

The market would bottom a few weeks later and rally well into August, only to tug optimists like myself under the surf once again, culminating in the bear's final bottom in October. Time after time, I thought things couldn't get any worse, and yet for the better part of a year, they did.

The sleepless nights, the anxious calls from clients, and the recriminations (sometimes nasty) from market bears were indelibly etched into my psyche as an investor. It was an experience I don't care to repeat, and one that forced me to learn a few new lessons about the new Wall Street. But more than anything, it forced me to relearn a few investment lessons I never should have forgotten.

In the weeks and months following that endless summer of 2002, I made a conscious effort to think about the causes and consequences of one of the most severe bear markets since the 1930s. The soul-searching investment essays I wrote for our institutional clients provided the raw material for this book. As a sell-side strategist, I spend between 70 and 80 days a year on the road visiting our institutional clients across the country and around the world. Good sell-side strategists are seldom shy and thrive on these meetings as a chance to show off their wares, to gain greater insight into what is and what isn't reflected in stock prices, and, most importantly, to gain insights from many of the world's best professional investors. But in those dark days in late 2002, my meetings with clients were rarely as much fun as they had been in the past, and often took on the tone of confusion, anger, and despair.

1973–1974 Revisited

With the exception of the 1929–1932 period, the greatest bear market in the modern era occurred in 1973–1974, when a combination of extended stock valuations, an oil shock, and a constitutional crisis in the United States all converged to bring the S&P down 48.2 percent over the course of 651 days.

When I first started in the business in the late 1980s, people would talk about the great '73–'74 bear market in hushed tones, the way one might talk about an earthquake or hurricane. Everyone knew it could happen again, but few expected to be in the middle of it. Then came October 1987, a frightening reminder of how quickly stock prices could fall. But for all of its drama, the '87 crash ended quickly, with the market actually posting gains in 1988. In fact, the market stabilized so quickly that retail and professional investors alike were largely able to avoid the painful self-introspection and greater regulatory scrutiny that often follow such major market declines. As a result, the great bull market that started in August 1982 proceeded largely uninterrupted, in spirit if not always in price, until the market peaked in March 2000.

But the decline that started in 2000 rivaled the 1973–1974 bear in magnitude (down 49.1 percent from peak to trough) and far exceeded it in duration (see Table I-1, below). Time and repetition are critical elements in changing human behavior, and the 929 days that passed between the market's peak on March 10, 2000, and its low on October 9, 2002, frequently put the lie to the new era thinking that so dominated economic and financial discussions in the late 1990s. So while the economic circumstances that accompanied the 2000–2002 bear market were vastly different from those witnessed in the 1973–1974 period, the impact of the market's decline on investor psychology and financial regulation were largely the same.

TABLE I-1   Bear Market Durations and Decline

			S&P 500
1973–1974	Starts:	January 11, 1973	**120.2**
	Ends:	October 23, 1973	**62.3**
	Magnitude:	−48.2%	
	Duration:	651 days	
2000–2001	Starts:	March 24, 2000	**1527.5**
	Ends:	October 9, 2002	**776.8**
	Magnitude:	−49.1%	
	Duration:	929 days	

Fear and anger have long been natural extensions of historic market declines. The Dow didn't surpass its 1929 peak, after all, until 1954. The recent scandals and the excesses in corporate America and on Wall Street have clearly shaken the average investor's confidence in common stocks and provided fertile ground for regulators and prosecutors to push for reform. Our recent collective experience during the bear market argues for greater caution and greater regulation. But private investors should remember that it has never paid to short America, and that the United States remains a beacon of freedom and opportunity. Public officials, on the other hand, need to remember that while it's important to throw the bad guys in jail, it isn't necessary to throw the baby out with the bathwater.

While stocks remain the most attractive and efficient way to build wealth for investors, the historic bubble in stock prices that took place in the late 1990s is unlikely to be repeated in the next several generations and requires a renewed focus on old investment lessons and a new approach to looking at common stocks and the financial markets. This book will attempt to make sense of this brave new world for investors and help them profit from the challenges and opportunities presented in a post bubble environment.

The first half of *New Markets, New Strategies* examines the major investment themes that grew out of the bear market and that I believe will shape the debates in the financial markets in the decade ahead. Chief among them will be a greater reliance on tried-and-true dividends to boost total return. A casualty of longstanding discriminatory tax treatment and the "it's different this time" approach to investing in common stocks in the late 1990s, a combination of lower average returns and a renewed emphasis on corporate governance would likely be, in and of themselves, powerful reasons for investors to reemphasize the importance of yield. President Bush's landmark 2003 tax cut on both dividends and capital gains only makes the after-tax return on stocks that much more attractive.

Also a function of the bear market (and incidentally, an all-time low in dividend yields) has been the rapid growth in hedge funds and alternative investments. In Chapter 2 we'll explore the nature and function of these largely unregulated and sometimes mysterious investment vehicles. No longer the province of elite money managers and wealthy individuals, hedge funds are having a greater impact on the market's volatility, are making traditional sentiment indictors less useful, and are changing the way money is managed among traditional "long only" investors. Their influence on the day-to-day functioning of the markets should not be underestimated.

Next we'll examine how the events of 9/11 and their aftermath have shaped government policy and why what happens in Washington will be increasingly relevant for investors in the decade ahead. Like it or not, we live in a world marked by greater violence and geopolitical risk. The horrific events of 9/11 have set a course for government policy and military spending that investors can't afford to ignore. The relationship between government policy and the financial markets has always been greater than many strategists would like to admit. In Chapter 3 we'll examine why what happens in Washington will have a greater influence on sector and stock selection than ever before.

The backlash from investors and regulators in the aftermath of the grizzly bear market that started in 2000 underscored once again how important it is to consider the character of those entrusted with managing the companies in which investors place their trust and money. In Chapter 4 we'll discuss why investing in good corporate governance will be crucial in the decade ahead for both the individual and institutional investor. We'll also provide a framework for investors to evaluate which boards and managements understand and respect the investor and those that do not.

In Chapter 5, the last investment theme we'll explore in Part I is the growing differences between winners and losers in today's modern global economy. Outperforming the broader market in recent years has had more to do with avoiding the worst stocks than picking the best ones. In such an environment, it will be increasingly important to consider the consequences of free trade and technological innovation on companies, workers, and investors,

In Part II we'll use the themes explored in the first half of *New Markets, New Strategies* to build a framework suitable for both the investment professional and the private investor.

In many ways the ever-increasing volatility of the financial markets in recent years is only a symptom of the increasingly fast-paced nature of modern life. Because stocks are, after all, long-term investments, the rapidity with which information is disseminated via the Internet and the 24-hour news cycle presents particular opportunities and pitfalls for investors. In Chapter 6 we'll explore the reasons why Wall Street analysts have developed such a bad reputation and how both professional and private investors alike will be able to profit from the return of unbiased and independent research in the years to come.

Of all the investment strategies and tactics that have been widely employed throughout the years, the contrarian approach has arguably been the most successful, albeit the most difficult to follow emotionally. Eschewing groupthink and crowd behavior is never easy, but it now appears obvious that the professional and private investor alike should have been selling stocks at the height of euphoria in March 2000 and buying stocks at the depths of despair in October 2002. In Chapter 7, Old Lord Keynes will once again show us that, when it comes to the contrarian approach, what is old is new again on today's new Wall Street.

The massive losses that accrued to investors in common stocks after the bubble burst have undoubtedly taught investors that good companies can often turn out to be bad investments. In Chapter 8 we'll discuss the importance of valuation in creating a long-term investment strategy, providing a straightforward approach to comparing companies across sectors.

In the last two chapters we'll attempt to bring all of these concepts together to provide a plan for both the investor who wishes to pick stocks and the investor who is likely to stick with mutual funds. While the investment objectives and time horizons of those reading this book will likely vary dramatically, my Thrifty Fifty portfolio as highlighted in Chapter 9 should provide meaningful insights into how investment professionals attempt to bridge the gap between big picture investment themes and the stock selection process. Finally, for those more comfortable with investing in mutual funds, we'll lay out the case for active management over indexation.

Throughout the following pages and chapters, you'll notice that I will at times use the first person narrative to relate anecdotes and personal perspectives about the various issues facing investors today. While this is generally considered outré in academic circles, I am no academic and believe it's important to draw bright lines between empirical research and personal opinion. Given the misconceptions that have been perpetuated in recent years about sell-side research analysts, I also believe that some of the stories of my travels as a Wall Street strategist will provide greater understanding of the challenges faced by people charged with giving investment professionals advice on how to manage other people's money.

Part I

≈

INVESTMENT THEMES FOR THE NEXT DECADE

1

YIELD MAKES A COMEBACK, AND THE IMPORTANCE OF DIVIDENDS

"Do you know the only thing that gives me pleasure? It's to see my dividends coming in."

—JOHN D. ROCKEFELLER, 1901

Imagine a Private Company

Imagine a friend of yours, the owner of a famous restaurant, comes to you with an exciting business opportunity. For a mere $50,000 he'll allow you to buy 5 percent of one of the most visibly successful businesses in town. While you've been waiting for an opportunity like this to build wealth for you and your family your whole life, you learn there's only one catch—you will receive no interest on the money you've invested and will not share in the business' profits. Of course, you'll be able to see audited financial statements from time to time, but they are financial statements your friend has personally constructed. And while your investment in this hot and trendy new restaurant will give you great cachet on the cocktail party circuit, your only real chance of earning a return on your investment will come when your friend, and your friend alone, decides to sell the business.

Sound appealing? Not on your life. But the stark scenario laid out above is roughly equivalent to buying publicly traded companies that pay no dividends. The example is not exactly fair because shares in public companies can be traded every second of the day between

9

9:30 a.m. and 4:00 p.m. But the point remains the same: Investments made in ventures that provide no regular return require almost complete faith and confidence in those who manage them. Given what we've all learned about the seedier side of runaway boards of directors and megalomaniacal CEOs, this prospect should appear less than appealing to anyone who's read a newspaper in the last four years.

The Historical Importance of Dividends

For anyone over 50 there must be a certain irony in reading the above subtitle, for as any first-year MBA student was once taught, dividend payments and earnings are the fundamental pillars upon which stock valuations are built. For the veteran investor, it might as well read: "The Historical Importance of Food." But the question remains: Why should one care about dividends when any investor even mentioning the term would have been summarily dismissed from any self-respecting growth conference only three years ago?

To be sure, the average 2 percent dividend yield of the S&P 500 from 1995 to 1999 was a mere afterthought in a period where the average total return was 26.3 percent. But, as Table 1-1 shows, the paltry contribution of dividends to the total return of large capitalization stocks in those years was the exception, not the rule, in the history of stock market returns. As a matter of fact, the contribution of dividends to the market's total return was nearly 75 percent in the 1940s and 1970s, falling to less than 25 percent by the 1990s. Perhaps more important, dividends have provided nearly half (that's right, half) of the total return on large cap stocks.

Conceptually, all investors would be well advised to remember that common stocks represent shares of a business rather than a high-class proxy for Lotto. The present value of any asset is equal to the value of all future cashflows discounted by some generally acceptable interest rate. As such, cash payments, rather than earnings themselves, are far more relevant to the process of valuing common stocks. Professor Jeremy Siegel of the Wharton School and author of the seminal work on investing in the modern era, *Stocks for the Long Run*, put it this way:

> **... the price of the stock is always equal to the present value of all future dividends and not the present value of future earnings. Earnings not paid to investors can have value only if they are paid as dividends or other cash disbursements at a late date. Valuing stocks at the present discounted value of future earn-**

TABLE 1-1   Dividends as a Percentage of Total Return

	PRICE % CHANGE	DIVIDEND CONTRIBUTION	TOTAL RETURN	DIVIDENDS % TOT RETURN	AVERAGE PAYOUT RATIO
1940s	34.8%	100.3%	135.0%	74.3	59.4
1950s	256.7%	180.0%	436.7%	41.2	54.6
1960s	53.7%	54.2%	107.9%	50.2	56.0
1970s	17.2%	59.1%	76.4%	77.4	45.5
1980s	227.4%	143.1%	370.5%	38.6	48.6
1990s	315.7%	95.5%	411.2%	23.2	47.6

ings is manifestly wrong and greatly overstates the value of a firm unless all the earnings are always paid out as dividends.[1]

Before the age of the SEC and audited financial statements, dividends were *the* way investors could determine whether the companies in which they were invested were actually making money. Still, despite the basic precepts of finance, common sense, and the historical record, only 360 of the companies within the vaunted S&P 500 Index even bothered to pay a dividend by the time President George W. Bush signed his historic tax cut in May 2003. How backward was our tax code? While I was never able to substantiate the claim, one of my clients told me that in 2003 the United States and Myanmar were the only two remaining countries in the world that taxed dividends twice with no offsets.

Two Percent Dividend Yields: Who's to Blame?

By March 2000, at the peak of the public's fascination with common stocks, the dividend yield on the broader market fell to an all-time low of 1.6 percent (see Chart 1-1). While a renewed focus on capital gains over dividends was collateral damage of the New Era thinking that so dominated the Internet boom in the late 1990s, long-standing government policies, shortsighted corporate management, shareholder apathy, and misguided academics all played a role in the dividend's fall from grace.

Of all the reasons dividends fell so out of favor with investors as a basis for total return, the most important was undoubtedly the discriminatory tax treatment of cash dividends vis-à-vis capital gains. In a somewhat remarkable sign of government acquisitiveness, sharehold-

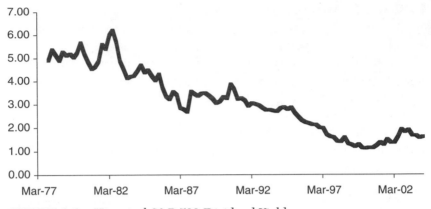

CHART 1-1 Historical S&P 500 Dividend Yield

ers have long been forced to pay taxes on corporate profits twice—
once when companies pay taxes on their earnings and again when
those earnings are distributed to shareholders. By the 1990s most
investors favored long-term capital gains, which were taxed at 20 percent, over dividends, which were taxed as ordinary income (in many
cases close to 50 percent.) In this regard, it was little wonder that both
management and investors favored less reliable and more volatile capital gains over humdrum dividends.

Given the stomach-churning declines in stock prices in the
2000–2002 period, one might be tempted to ask where were the
boards of directors, and why were managements so callous in their
treatment of shareholders? The recent spate of stories on executive
abuses might make it easy to assume that management was complicit
in a system to separate investors from their money. And while some
CEOs undoubtedly used the double taxation of dividends as a con-
venient cover for their empire-building odysseys (think Tyco), more
often than not companies have been fearful that the Street would
brand them as unsophisticated Old Economy rubes if they provided
income to their shareholders rather than engaging in deals that created investment banking fees.

Until the passage of President Bush's landmark tax cut on dividends
and capital gains in May 2003, the tax laws largely discouraged managements from providing a cash return to investors and increasingly
forced them to get on the Wall Street earnings treadmill every quarter by using shareholders' hard-fought earnings to open up new stores
and to enter businesses and offer products for which they had no

competitive edge or expertise. A laundry list of failed mergers and serial acquirers from these years now stands in the wake of that disturbing trend.

Shareholders, of course, were not without blame for the decreasing importance of yield. It would seem the height of naivety for anyone to expect companies to provide dividends until investors themselves start to demand them, and for the most part, individual and institutional investors alike were largely silent on the subject. Regardless of the motivations behind the focus on capital gains, the end result was the same—investors were left with suboptimal returns.

Of course, no blight upon the landscape of common sense could be complete without the participation of the academic community. With regard to dividend policy, the assault came from Franco Modigliani of MIT and Merton Miller of the University of Chicago, both Nobel Prize winners, who argued that in a world without taxes, transaction costs, or other market imperfections, dividend policy was largely irrelevant for corporate finance decisions. Despite the Fantasy Island assumptions upon which their theories were based, their work was used as the basis for the argument, often heard in the late '90s, that companies should pay the lowest cash dividend possible whenever dividends were taxed more heavily than capital gains. A more modern interpretation of their work suggests that taxes play an important role in corporate finance decisions.[2]

Case Study: McDonald's

As I suffered through an endless summer of corporate scandal and blood on the Street, I knew that I needed to revisit some of these old lessons on stock valuation. An In-N-Out Burger may seem to be a strange setting for an epiphany on dividends, but a foray to the venerable fast food chain while on a trip to visit our West Coast clients in the summer of 2002 seemed to provide greater clarity on the subject, and on other corporate finance dilemmas, than the variety of corporate perp walks and ambush interviews then ubiquitous on CNBC.

While I had long been a fast food aficionado, I was surprised to find a business that stood in stark contrast to what one might find at McDonald's—the staff was courteous and efficient, the lines were fast-moving, and, perhaps most surprisingly, there were only three items on the menu: burgers, fries, and soda. A sign near the entrance announced that there were employment opportunities for $8.25 an hour. Like reporters, good sell-side analysts are always looking for material, and this seemed to be such a wide departure from the traditional fast food model that I thought it was worthy of further study.

As I waited for my order, I started to muse about the contrast between the simplicity of the In-N-Out operation and McDonald's, which expanded from its modest roots to sell everything from salads to toys and then planned to open an additional 1,300 to 1,400 new restaurants on a global basis (a target, incidentally, the company described as "modest"). This would have been all well and good if not for the dismal return McDonald's had provided investors in the prior several years. Remarkably at that time, "Burgers," as it is affectionately known on Wall Street, had underperformed the S&P in price terms by nearly 25 percent since the start of 1990. To add insult to injury, I learned that the company's average annual dividend yield was only 0.8 percent in 2001 despite generating nearly $2.23 per share in free cashflow. Falling to nearly $15 a share by the end of 2002, the company still sported a below-market dividend yield of only 1.2 percent.

Certainly it might have been unfair to compare the performance of a large public company with a small and privately held one. But it seemed clear to me that the returns McDonald's shareholders could have achieved could have been higher had the company followed the Snyder family's lead and managed the company for income and yield and rather than capital gains, as McDonald's had.

How did McDonald's get into this mess? In my opinion it was an overwhelming desire reinforced by the sell-side to be a growth stock at all costs, whether or not the expected return on retained earnings was attainable. The dividend yield suffered and blue chip investors abandoned the stock indexes. And McDonald's was not unique in its quest to satisfy the Wall Street earnings machine at the expense of cash disbursements. After the peak, weak top-line growth and the discriminatory tax treatment of dividends had prompted corporate managements to choose share repurchases over dividends as a better way to enhance shareholder value to shareholders.

The good news is that McDonald's finally got the message. Under the stewardship of Jim Cantalupo, the company scaled back its expansion plans, focused on its core business, and increased its dividend. After languishing for years, McDonald's stock price rose from $16 to over $27 in 2004.

Dividends and Growth Stocks

Even after three consecutive years of declines for the broader market, old habits die hard. Despite ample evidence that there is more to a stock's return than price and a game-changing tax cut, some managements and shareholders remain skeptical of the importance of dividends. I am continually amazed in my travels that individual and institutional investors alike remain fascinated with capital gains to the exclusion of yield. The principal objection to companies actually providing a return to their shareholders, often perpetuated by managements themselves, is that companies that pay dividends are tacitly suggesting they can no longer grow earnings quickly enough to justify growth stock multiples.

Although it is impossible to know for sure, this seemed to be at least part of the reason Microsoft, the poster child for large cap growth stocks, was so unwilling to share some of its cash hoard with investors in the form of a dividend. As the bubble burst, however, there were some signs that the company's stinginess was wearing thin: By 2001 a group of Microsoft shareholders and analysts led by muckraker and quadrennial presidential candidate Ralph Nader had started to call for the technology company to change its dividend policy.[3]

Things started to change in the fall of 2002 when President Bush spoke about the long harmful practice of double-taxing dividends. Perhaps the President's proposal to end this widely maligned policy and Microsoft's decision to pay its first ever dividend in October of that year was a coincidence, but it seems unlikely. Whatever the rationale for the company's change of heart, the Bush administration quickly pointed to the decision as evidence of the dividend proposal's potential salutary effect on corporate governance. It should be mentioned that many wondered whether Mister Softy's decision to provide some regular return to its investors actually "opened the kimono" on the company's diminished growth prospects. But with more than $40 billion in cash on its balance sheet at the time, most Microsoft shareholders had long since accepted the fact that the company was no longer in its hypergrowth phase.

While the natural tension between dividends and the growth stock culture won't be quelled for some years to come, recent academic research suggests that companies that pay dividends have actually had higher long-term growth in earnings. In essence, being a dividend payer and a growth stock need not be mutually exclusive. In the

January/February 2003 issue of the *Financial Analysts Journal*, Robert Arnott and Clifford Asness wrote their seminal work on the subject, "Surprise! Higher Dividends = Higher Earnings Growth." In it, the authors observed that expected future earnings growth is fastest when current payout ratios are high, and slowest when payout ratios are low. The authors postulated that this was due to the fact that dividends provide important signals about a company's confidence in its ability to generate earnings and cashflow in the future. Further, a greater reliance on the public markets to fund growth, rather than retained earnings, imposes a welcome dose of financial sobriety and reality on capital spending and acquisition decisions.[4]

While there is still a significant amount of residual skepticism about the relationship between growth stocks and dividends, there are some hopeful signs that paying a dividend does not impugn the long-term growth prospects of traditional growth stocks like Microsoft and Qualcomm.

Lowering the Tax Rate on Dividends and Capital Gains

Given the fact that the unemployment rate for the U.S. economy had increased from an all-time low of 3.8 percent in 2000 to over 6 percent in 2002, it was more than a little impressive to me that the President, after two prior income tax cuts, put the end of the double taxation of dividends at the forefront of his 2003 tax cut. Without wanting to sound cynical, it was one of the few widely publicized instances I can remember in which a politician proposed legislation on its merits regardless of the political fallout. I think it took a lot of guts for a Republican President (whose father, incidentally, was ousted in part for his alleged apathy to the economic plight of the little guy) to propose a policy that he had to know some in the media and on Capitol Hill would label a "tax cut for the rich." But while there were big debates about the priority given to the tax cut on dividends and whether the tax cut should have been at the corporate rather than the individual level, few professional economists criticized the plan on its academic merits.

Although ISI's Washington team, led by Tom Gallagher, believed the President's proposal to end the double taxation of dividends in October 2002 had a decent chance of making it through Congress, the plan was met with scorn, if not open hostility, in some provinces of

Washington and Wall Street. And despite the Republicans' impressive showing in the 2002 mid-term elections, there were a number of times the President's proposal looked as if it would never reach his desk.[5]

But persistence on the part of the administration and the military successes on the ground in Iraq, at the time, combined to give the President the votes he needed to get his tax package through Congress. Although I may be biased because he is a friend, Larry Kudlow, former Reagan administration economist and co-host of the popular CNBC program Kudlow & Cramer, was tireless in his efforts to explain the economic rationale for this historic change. As recounted in the *New York Times*, "All summer long on his program, which is watched by White House officials (although not President Bush), Mr. Kudlow hammered at the idea of dividend tax cuts. At the same time, conservative economists kept up the pressure on the White House."[6] In signing the Jobs and Growth Act of 2003 in a Rose Garden ceremony on May 28, 2003, President Bush was able to bring the tax rate on dividends and capital gains down to 15 percent.

For those investors who suffered through the '60s and '70s, the drop in tax rates on investment was almost too good to be true. At the time, I remember ISI's vice chairman, Jim Moltz—former chairman of the board of the legendary Wall Street research boutique C.J. Lawrence, and a board member of the New York Stock Exchange—saying to me, "Jason, do you realize that when I started in this business in 1955, the top marginal income tax rate was over 90 percent, and that when you were still in diapers [not really] the top rate on capital gains was over 50 percent?" His point was clear: With 15 percent tax rates on dividends and capital gains, this was one of the most attractive environments to own stocks on an after-tax basis since the federal income tax was introduced in 1913 (see Chart 1-2).

Potential Impact of the Tax Cut

Not only did the Jobs and Growth Act of 2003 bring the blended tax rate on stock ownership to its lowest levels in nearly 70 years, it also had major implications for corporate finance decisions and the increasing importance of corporate governance issues.

Perhaps the most deleterious effect of the discriminatory tax treatment of dividends had been the preference of companies to issue debt and retain earnings to fund acquisitions and capital spending programs. Every business school in the country has taught future

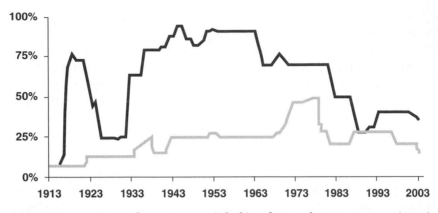

CHART 1-2 Top Ordinary Income (Black) and Capital Gains Tax Rate (Gray)

financial managers that, because interest costs rather than dividend payments are tax deductible for the corporation, debt capital is far cheaper than equity capital.

As a result, companies thought they could lower their cost of capital by borrowing more under the old tax regime. As a result, managements retained earnings and raised excessive levels of debt. This proclivity is not inconsequential in the history of the bubble and its aftermath—the growth in aggregate debt levels of both the public and in corporate America was in many ways the single greatest reason massive fiscal and monetary stimulus took so long to take hold. Not only did it hurt long-term returns for investors, it also encouraged poor corporate finance decisions, like bad acquisitions and ill-timed capital spending decisions.

The Jobs and Growth Act reversed a lot of these distortions and has resulted in what appears to be a real sea change in dividend policy. It is still safe to say that many investors remain skeptical that the decline in the tax rate on dividends will result in any significant change in dividend policy. And there are plenty of examples of managements who still don't "get it." But according to data released by S&P, it appears that companies are indeed taking the administration's lead on the issue.

In 2003 there were 247 instances within the S&P 500 of companies initiating or increasing their dividends, a big increase over 2002. As Chart 1-3 indicates, nearly 40 percent of those actions have occurred since the President's tax package was signed into law. Perhaps more significant, the average amount of dividend increases has been 24 percent since the law went into effect, versus 18 percent over 2003. The Financials and Information Technology sectors have been the biggest contributors to this trend. Thus far, at least concerning the effect of the law on dividends, the President ought to be pleased.

But despite signs that managements are starting to realize the benefits of dividends, investor apathy toward dividend-paying stocks was one of the great mysteries in 2003. Oddly, they underperformed stocks that paid no dividends last year. Antidividend investors and managements have cited this as proof that the administration's tax cut gambit wasn't worth the effort. But I believe we need far more time to evaluate the new policy's impact.

While every strategist on the Street has a reason as to why dividend payers underperformed their more profligate competition for investor funds in 2003, there are two explanations that stand out among the others. First and foremost, shareholders of common stocks had been conditioned over an entire decade to look at returns in price terms only. Most investors who started buying stocks in the decade of the 1990s became spoiled with the seemingly perpetual 20-percent-plus returns and thus never realized that there was a yield component to total return. As such, it will take far more than a year for investors to start to notice the impact higher dividends and payout ratios are having on their returns.

The second reason has to do with the cut in the capital gains tax rate from 20 to 15 percent. Remarkably, this tax cut was rarely mentioned in the sometimes heated debates that led to the Jobs and Growth Act

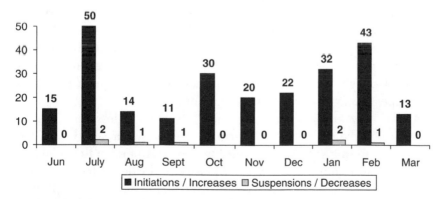

CHART 1-3 Changes in Dividend Policy by S&P 500 Companies Following Passage of 2003 Bush Tax Cut

of 2003. It essentially sneaked into the final bill. When combined with the administration's 2002 tax cuts, which accelerated depreciation schedules and gave incentives for companies to purchase new equipment, tech stocks took off, leaving the more staid dividend payers behind.

Eventually, we hope that the game on Wall Street will center on handicapping the next company that currently pays no dividend but is about to. ("Psst, I hear Tom Siebel's holding a press conference." "Really? What's the symbol?") Certainly, a number of companies, like Microsoft and casino operator Mandalay Bay, have felt compelled to share some of the profits with their owners. With over $2 trillion in low-yielding money market funds, however, I believe that over time many investors will gravitate toward large, stable companies that offer the prospect of a growing stream of tax-advantaged income.

While the equal tax rates on dividends and capital gains made it difficult to discern investor preferences among equities in the short term, there can be little doubt about investor preferences between equities and bonds. Why? If one takes a look at Table 1-2, in which I assume a 40 percent tax rate, the historical 7 percent yearly increase in earnings, and a 2 percent dividend yield, and compare the increase in return to an investor in bonds versus stocks due to the new tax laws, it becomes clear that the marginal benefit is clearly to the investor in common stocks. As a matter of fact, the theoretical return on stocks is 12.5 percent higher after the cut in dividends and capital gains, versus no change in return to a bondholder.

While changes in dividend policy, the attitude toward retained earnings, and the impact on investor preferences are meaningful, perhaps more important is the potential impact the tax cut on dividends might have on corporate governance. The idea that the mere act of paying a dividend leads to more responsive managements was summed up eloquently by Michael Goldstein, a finance professor at Babson College: "Dividends are good because they remind the CEO four times a year that it's not his company."[7]

As we now know, some companies resorted to less than ethical means to "make the numbers" during those heady days in the bubble years. Accounting scandals are nothing new to American financial history, to be sure, but the reduced emphasis on dividends has undoubtedly exacerbated them. As we'll discuss in the last chapter, a lower-than-average nominal growth environment, heavy debt burdens on the part of both consumers and corporations, and rising budget

TABLE 1-2 2003 Dividend Tax Cut and After-Tax Return

		Old Tax Code			New Tax Code			Change
		Return	1 minus Tax Rate	After-Tax Return	Return	1 minus Tax Rate	After Tax Return	
Bonds	Total	4.00%	0.61	2.44%	4.00%	0.65	2.60%	4.48%
Stocks	Earnings	7.00%	0.8	5.60%	7.00%	0.85	5.95%	
	Dividends	2.00%	0.61	1.22%	2.00%	0.85	1.70%	
	Total			6.82%			7.65%	12.17%

deficits might make double-digit price returns difficult to come by over the next several years. By extension, it seems logical that dividends will likely be seen as a more important part of an investment's total return. More and more shareholders are realizing that while it's relatively easy to fudge operating earnings numbers, a dividend check is hard to fake. A renewed emphasis on dividends should go a long way in restoring investor confidence.

The Future

Despite all the back-biting and doubt that accompanied the Jobs and Growth Act, it could be that the tax had some meaningful impact on economic growth (real GDP rose at 8.2 percent in the third quarter of 2003) and the performance of stocks (the S&P has risen 17 percent since the package was passed).

Still, there are some who wonder how we can grow the economy while at the same time returning to shareholders a portion of profits that is rightfully theirs. Looking at the historical payout ratio (the portion of net income actually returned to shareholders), you will see that, at 35 percent, it's at the lowest level in more than 60 years (Table 1-3). And since dividend payments as a percentage of cashflow are now at all-time lows, companies have plenty of room to increase their dividends *and* fund new capital investment.

Another question that remains in this brave new world of dividend policy is whether investors will continue to favor capital gains over yield. While it's always dangerous to predict the nature of crowds, Australia's experience with dividend reform might provide an interesting guide.

In the mid-1980s, Australia made sweeping changes to its tax policy with regard to capital gains and dividends. In 1985, a capital gains

TABLE 1-3	Average Dividend Payout Ratio
1940s	74.3%
1950s	41.2%
1960s	50.4%
1970s	77.4%
1980s	38.6%
1990s	23.2%

tax was introduced; in 1987, Australian investors could take a tax credit for any income tax paid by the company on the income from which dividends were derived; and in 1988, superannuation funds (government mandated retirement funds) were entitled to a rebate from income tax payable from the full amount of the imputation credit attached to the dividends. Some academic studies suggested that, after all was said and done, shareholders continued to prefer capital gains after the change.[8] While this is somewhat disappointing to fans of dividends, like myself, it is also interesting to note that the performance of the Australia All Ordinaries index outperformed the S&P 500 during this time period.

Certainly, a renewed focus on dividends and a tax code that creates incentives to provide them could go a long way in creating better corporate finance decisions and better returns for investors. There is a sense in which Microsoft's decision to pay a dividend may very well add the term "blue chip" to the lexicon of a whole new generation of investors. The absence of dividends in the '90s removed an essential safety net for investors in common stocks. And for companies that perpetually underperformed, one wonders how much more interest there might have been in a McDonald's that yielded 4 percent rather than 1 percent, as cited in our fast food case study.

Already low interest rates and relatively full valuations are likely to cause investors to view dividends as a more important part of a stock's total return. With the major averages essentially flat over the past six years, one wonders whether managements or shareholders themselves would have been better allocators of capital. And while few argue that companies should have the flexibility to retain earnings for important capital spending projects and strategic acquisitions, the last few years have taught all of us as shareholders that the bar for such decisions ought to be higher. In this regard, the change in the tax treatment of dividends just might have changed everything. Let's hope both management and shareholders pay heed to the lessons of the past and remember that yield has been an important part of the total return for investors.

A Note on Preferreds

It might be tempting to look to preferred issues with relatively high yields to take advantage of the new tax laws. And although there has been a lot of excitement about the potential boost to preferred issues under the new tax regime, investors need to be careful. My discussions with experts in the field have warned me that few preferreds issued after 1995 would likely be subject to the tax change because of their structures. Some preferred securities aren't really preferred equity structures at all but would most likely be considered subordinated debt instruments held by a trust. That means they pay interest instead of dividends, and would therefore be ineligible for the preferred tax treatment. Look before you leap.

Key Take-Aways

1. Owning stocks should not be considered the same as buying a Lotto ticket. Shares represent ownership in business.
2. Earnings and dividends are the most transparent way to determine a company's success.
3. Dividends have historically been a major contributor to the total return of common stocks.
4. Last year's tax cuts on dividends and capital gains now make the blended tax rate on dividends lower now than it has been in almost 70 years.
5. Paying a dividend and being a growth company are not inconsistent. In fact, companies that pay dividends have actually had higher earnings growth rates throughout time.
6. Dividends lead to better corporate governance decisions and greater respect for shareholders.
7. Not all preferred stocks will be eligible for the cuts in dividend tax rates.

2

THE GROWING INFLUENCE OF HEDGE FUNDS

WALL STREET'S BIGGEST CUSTOMERS

"O speculators about perpetual motion, how many vain chimeras have been created in the like quest? Go and take your place with the seekers after gold."
—LEONARDO DA VINCI

The Third Rail of Investment Strategy

I can tell by the nervous laughter and the eye rolls from my firm's institutional salesmen that talking about hedge funds has become the third rail of sell-side investment strategy. While, as we will see, the first hedge fund was created over 50 years ago, their growing influence on the money management industry and on the financial market is relatively new. Currently Wall Street's largest customers, candid discussions about the influence these investment pools are having on the broader market are often conspicuously absent from most investment research and media coverage. This is unfortunate for those both inside and outside the alternative investment industry who wish to make sense of the market's broader trends.

Long vilified in much the same way as the speculators and robber barons of old, hedge funds have all too often been scapegoats for economic difficulties and market dislocations that had their roots in poor valuations and flawed public policies. Largely absent from any discussion of the subject is the positive influence hedge funds are having on the fee and compensation structure of the money management industry at large.

But as the events surrounding the crisis at Long Term Capital Management in 1998 so vividly pointed out, it is difficult to determine whether the promises of the hedge fund structure—to provide decent low risk absolute returns year in and year out—have been met. The answer to this question is made even more difficult because the industry has grown from a small group of elite professional investors to a large and amorphous group of firms with varying degrees of skill and experience. Indeed, as we will see, the growth of alternative investments has been so rapid that few within the industry itself understand the outsized influence they themselves are having on the financial markets.

The industry's critics have suggested that these speculative pools are overleveraged, unregulated, and disruptive to the world's financial markets. Its defenders are quick to point out that the hedge fund structure puts the interests of the customer and the fund manager on the same plane. As with most polemics concerning financial markets, the truth lies somewhere in between. But the growth and size of the industry is now so large that few investors, individual or professional, can ignore the influence these pools are having on both the traditional money management business or on the workings of the financial markets at large.

So What's a Hedge Fund?

No discussion of the growing influence of hedge funds on the investment landscape would be complete without first trying to define them. A quick search on the Internet would yield almost as many different definitions of these sometimes mysterious investment pools as there are funds themselves. While relatively lax regulatory oversight and the sheer individuality of those attracted to the industry make any general definition difficult, the best way to describe hedge funds may be to differentiate them from their distant cousins in the mutual fund industry.

First and foremost, hedge funds are flexible. While mutual funds are usually precluded from trading on the short side or are limited to the amount of leverage that can be employed, hedge funds have no such restrictions. Although there are hedge funds that specialize in everything from bond arbitrage to currencies, the rapid growth in the industry has most significantly and recently been felt in the fairly bread-and-butter long/short equity fund.

Another significant difference between hedge funds and mutual funds is the way in which they charge for their services. While the typical mutual fund charges a set fee to compensate for fund management—on average, about 1 percent of assets under management—the hedge fund charges both a management fee, which normally amounts to between 1 and 3 percent of the assets under management, *and* an incentive fee, which normally amounts to 20 percent of the realized or unrealized profits of the fund. As we will see later in the chapter, the incentive fee is perhaps the most interesting, albeit controversial, feature of the hedge fund structure.

That leads to another key difference between mutual funds and hedge funds: their size. The rapidity with which capital must be employed to generate the types of returns that make a 20 percent incentive fee palatable means that hedge funds need to remain relatively small. The larger a fund becomes, the more likely its footprints in the marketplace will quickly eliminate any pricing inefficiencies the fund wishes to exploit. While a typical mutual fund might have hundreds of analysts and portfolio managers assigned to various subsegments of the market, the typical hedge fund employs from one to 20 analysts and traders. Very few employ more than 100. For example, the largest actively managed fund complex in the United States, Fidelity Management, had $770 billion under management as of October 2000. In contrast, the largest hedge funds manage less than $10 billion.

But perhaps the most important difference between the two structures remains a regulatory one. In the aftermath of the Crash of 1929 and the Great Depression, the federal government and the newly formed Securities and Exchange Commission outlawed the practice of money managers taking a percentage of gains as compensation for their services—forcing them, instead, to charge a fee. This gave birth to the modern day mutual fund model. But under the Investment Advisers Act of 1940, the government did allow unregulated pools of money to be managed, provided they had no more than 99 "accredited" or "wealthy" investors. While Depression era laws regulating the fund industry have largely kept hedge funds a province of those with means, the 1996 National Securities Markets Improvement Act removed some of the more onerous and arbitrary rules regarding those who met the definition of "accredited" and thus might need protection. The law greatly increased the ranks of hedge funds and those who might be eligible to invest in them.[1]

Finally, hedge funds are different from their mutual fund cousins in the liquidity they provide to their investors. While an investor in a mutual fund can liquidate his investment at the net asset value (NAV) of the fund at the close of trading each day, most hedge funds impose a "lockup" period of a year or more to allow the hedge fund manager greater flexibility in trading less liquid securities and to maximize the fund's capital at risk.

Given these differences with long-only money management firms, hedge funds can be broadly defined as: lightly regulated limited partnerships that can employ a variety of different investment tools, including leverage and short sales; trade in a variety of different financial products; and charge an incentive fee for their services.

Origins of the Present-Day Hedge Fund

Alfred W. Jones is generally believed to be the world's first hedge fund manager when he opened his eponymous firm with $100,000 in capital ($40,000 of it his own) in 1949. Given the mystery surrounding the hedge fund industry today, perhaps it's only fitting that its origins come from such an interesting and unlikely source.

Jones was not an overaggressive operator of an investment trust from the 1930s, but rather, an outsider and academic. Born in Australia to American parents, he graduated from Harvard in 1923, received a Ph.D. from Columbia in sociology, served his country as a foreign service officer in Berlin, and wound up reporting on the Spanish Civil War for Time Life publications in the 1940s. His thesis, *Life, Liberty, and Property*, is still used as a reference text in sociology to this day. The financial world was also of interest to Jones, and after writing a series of articles for *Fortune* on the size and structure of the asset management industry and the trends in investing and market forecasting, he became convinced that he could use the basic speculative tools of leverage and short sales to achieve conservative, and steady, investment returns.[2]

Originally formed as a general partnership to avoid the long gaze of the Securities and Exchange Commission, and to preserve the greatest possible flexibility in the construction of his portfolios, Jones conceived of an investment pool that used short sales to fund and to hedge its long positions. He deemed it a "hedged fund." Perhaps it's some measure of the man that he is reported to have been dismayed at the bastardization of the original term he used to describe his creation: "My original expression, and the proper one, was 'hedged fund.' I still regard 'hedge fund,' which makes a noun serve for an adjective, with distaste."[3]

By 1965, Jones showed a five-year gain of 325 percent and 10-year gain of almost 700 percent. More remarkable still, he nearly tripled the performance of the Dow Jones Industrial Average during a broadly constructive period for U.S. stocks. His record allowed Jones to devise the 20 percent incentive fee that remains the basis for hedge fund compensation today. Perhaps more interesting, Jones's limited partners were not of the rich and famous who so often populate the ranks of hedge fund investors today, but rather, they were of the intelligentsia. It was for this reason that, despite his notable success, Jones operated largely in anonymity until the mid-1960s, when Carol Loomis featured him in the pages of *Fortune*.

Jones's success and eventual notoriety provided fertile ground for new hedge funds (many Jones alumni) to grow. While data from that period is sketchy, a 1968 survey found that, out of the 215 investment partnerships in the country, 140 were probably hedge funds. What's more, some of the industry's brightest stars started hedge funds in this period, including Warren Buffett (Omaha-based Buffett Partners), Walter Schloss (WJS Partners), and George Soros (Quantum Fund).[4] The efficacy of these funds would later be put to the test in the 1969–1970 and 1973–1974 bear markets, but a new industry was born.

Jones remained a man apart to the last, using the significant wealth he amassed during his stewardship of the world's first hedge fund to embark on a personal crusade to end poverty in America. A fascinating epilogue to his life came in 1982, when, at 82 years of age, he amended his original partnership agreement to become a fund of funds.[5]

Size and Structure of the Hedge Fund Market

When I first started in the business in the late 1980s, hedge funds were reserved for wealthy individuals and were managed by a handful of mostly world-class and legendary investors, among them, George Soros, Julian Robertson, and Paul Tudor Jones. Today there are actually more hedge funds than mutual funds, although the assets of the latter dwarf those of the former.

According to the hedge fund consulting firm, Van Hedge, by 2003 there were roughly 8,000 hedge funds worldwide with assets of $650 billion. Given the fact that the hedge fund business only started to grow in earnest in 1990, these figures compare favorably with the roughly $7 trillion parked in the nation's 5,900 mutual funds. It may not sound like much money, but as Chart 2-1 shows, these figures represent an asymptotic rise from the $10 billion or so in hedge funds in 1991.

Despite the rapid rise, there are few signs that this phenomenon has run its course. Anecdotally and through my observations at our shop, it seems that talented money managers and analysts are breaking off from traditional firms and other hedge funds with greater and greater frequency.

One of the more interesting features of the industry's structure is its pricing. Hedge fund services are normally considered what economists would call a Giffen good—a rare type of product seldom seen in the real world, in which an increase in the price results in an increase in the quantity demanded. I once asked a good friend of mine in the hedge fund business why no one ever tried to compete on price—that is, why wouldn't a hedge fund accept less than the standard 1 percent management fee and 20 percent of the profits? His response: "No one would have any confidence in a manager who charged less."

At once amusing and accurate, this comment underscores the idea that throughout their history, hedge fund investments have been seen as a luxury good ruled by inelastic pricing. A Giffen good must be inferior to other available products to fully meet the true academic

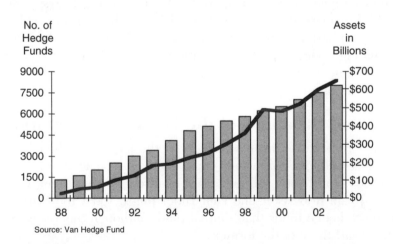

Source: Van Hedge Fund

CHART 2-1 Hedge Fund Assets and Number of Hedge Funds, 1988–2003

definition of the term, but the point largely remains the same: Investors are generally more interested in funds that charge higher fees. It should be noted, however, that this may start to change for hedge funds. Increased interest in alternative investments from some of the country's largest investment pools may force traditional money management companies to reconsider their fee structures and come up with new and innovative ways to price their services.

It is interesting to note that, paradoxically, old-line firms are now also starting to fuel the growth in alternative investments. Eager to boost revenues and profits, and desperate to hold onto their most talented players, investment banks and traditional money management firms are getting into the act, building hedge fund operations to go with their traditional areas of expertise.

Why the Growth in Hedge Fund Assets Is So Important

Few investors and journalists are neutral about the growth in the hedge fund industry. Long-only managers often see it as a blight upon the landscape of long-term investing, roiling markets and creating undue volatility. Hedge fund managers, in contrast, view themselves as the ultimate exemplification of free markets. "What better way is there," they ask, "than to compensate money managers than on performance rather than on assets under management?"

In the purpose of full disclosure, as a sell-sider interested in self-preservation, I never felt compelled to come down on either side of the issue. I do believe, however, that the growth in the hedge fund structure represents a seismic shift in the nature of money management and the industries that seek to service it. Regardless of one's feelings about hedge funds, there are a number of implications for the buy-side and sell-side alike.

Death of the Buy-and-Hold Strategy
Of all the industries ripe for consolidation in the United States, the money management and brokerage industries are near the top. Increasingly, traditional money management firms are forced to compete with hedge funds for assets and for talent. This process is undoubtedly being hastened by the fact that institutional investors, such as pension funds and endowments, are becoming more comfortable with alternative investment structures. As flows into equities have dried up in recent years, the competition for the marginal dollar has

intensified. Chasing performance has become the norm, turning traditionally staid mutual funds into gunslingers.

According to Bain & Co., the average holding period for stocks in the United States was eight years in 1960, versus 11 months in 2001 (see Chart 2-2). Practically speaking, a buy-and-hold strategy is becoming impossible for any fund manager who wants to hold onto his job. As a friend of mine who runs a mutual fund said, "I could get fired a lot of times in eight years." This focus on short-term performance has undoubtedly been good for brokers, but the question remains as to whether it has ultimately been in the best interests of shareholders. In terms of turnover and commission generation, some mutual funds are increasingly being operated like their hedge fund competition.

Paying for Performance Gains Traction

Despite new and persistent calls for regulation and concerns about performance, there is one element of the growth in hedge funds that suggests that it's in its second inning rather than its eighth: Increasingly, pension funds and endowments are carving out a portion of the funds earmarked for equities to alternative investments.

What is most attractive about hedge funds to these long-term investors is their desire for noncorrelated returns and, perhaps more important, the idea that fees are dependent upon performance. It remains to be seen how noncorrelated these returns will be, and whether a 1 percent management fee and a 20 percent performance

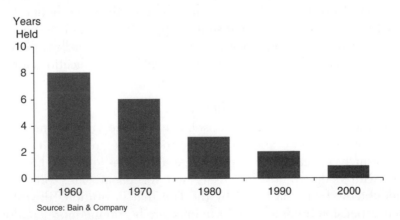

Source: Bain & Company

CHART 2-2 Average Holding Period (in Years) for Stocks by Decade fee is an appropriate fee structure for all hedge funds, regardless of size, historical performance, or reputation. And at least some investors have wondered whether such outsized fee structures encourage inordinate risk-taking. Still, mutual funds ought to take note of this relatively new way to pay for money management services.

An Industry "Brain Drain"

The growth in hedge funds and alternative investments is also shaping today's investment landscape because of the fledgling industry's mounting competition for analytical and trading talent. In much the same way that investment banks were able to attract the best and the brightest from commercial banks in the 1980s, hedge funds now provide a viable alternative to both the freshly minted MBA and the seasoned Wall Street professional.

At the same time, a significant drop in the payrolls of traditional Wall Street firms has made the siren call of significant incentive fees that much more appealing. Greater regulatory scrutiny, management control, and media criticism has started to wear thin among sell-side research analysts who have had their pay drop substantially in the past three years. In this regard, the intellectual flexibility and earnings potential hedge funds provide are tempting to the new breed of investment professional.

Although the comparison makes a lot of my friends in the hedge fund industry cringe, I believe the gold rush mentality of seeking employment at hedge funds is similar to the Internet boom in the late 1990s. While the hedge fund model is inherently more profitable than many of the Internet businesses that were floated in the boom, in much the same way, talented young people—often disenchanted with the slow pace of making it in traditional businesses—sought employment at fledgling Internet companies. Now, to complete the analogy, talented analysts and portfolio managers leave traditional buy-and-sell shops with the hopes of reaping untold millions.

The Influence of Commissions on Research

It wasn't too long ago when just about anyone on the sell-side—from the receptionist to the CEO—could have reeled off the names of the Street's top five customers: Fidelity, Alliance, American Express, and so on. Today, it's likely that neither the receptionist nor the CEO could come anywhere near naming their firm's best customers, because most didn't exist five years ago.

BusinessWeek recently reported that one of the country's most successful hedge funds generated over $150 million in commissions last year, making it one of the Street's top 10 customers despite having only $4 billion in assets. To put this number in perspective, Fidelity, traditionally considered the Street's largest customer, is reported to pay out just over $200 million a year in commissions, but has $1 trillion under management.

At best, typical institutional commission rates are about a nickel a share. At that rate, a firm would need to trade about 3 billion shares a year, or over 8 million shares a day, to generate $150 million a year in commissions. This is not easily done on an asset base of $4 billion. Though this may be some lurid fantasy of an overeager sales manager, it's hard to deny that trading volume from hedge funds has become so large that some sell-side firms have sprung up just to cater to them.

One should be wondering why a firm that has proven to be so successful at ferreting out profitable trades would need to trade so often. It's an interesting question, to which there are few easy answers. There is little question that most hedge funds feel they need to be more active to generate the types of returns expected by a 20 percent incentive fee. But increasingly it seems that outsized commission generation is part of the strategy hedge funds employ to get the "first call," and thus increase the chances of getting value-added research.

Jim Cramer, cohost of *Kudlow & Cramer* and founding partner of a very successful hedge fund in the late '80s and '90s, explained the importance of commissions to the hedge fund manager in his book *Confessions of a Street Addict*:

> **When I asked her how we could find out about all these wonderful things when I was just a little hedge fund manager, she said one word: "commish" … Commissions, she explained, determine what you are told, what you will know, and how much you can find out. If you do a massive amount of commission business, analysts will return your calls, brokers will work for you, and you will get plenty of ideas to make money on both a short and a long-term basis.[6]**

As a big fan of free markets, I see nothing wrong with the growing influence of hedge funds. But it is important for hedge fund and long-only managers alike to remember where the sell-side research analyst's bread is being buttered. The result of this shift in the balance of commission power will be the increasingly short-term nature of sell-side research. It is a major reason that investment banks are focusing so much attention on technical analysis and pairs trades. There is, of course, nothing wrong with this. But long-term investors should know who the sell-side's best customers are.

The Declining Usefulness of Traditional Sentiment Indicators

In 2002, bears often pointed to the exceedingly bullish levels of sentiment indicators such as *MarketVane, Investors Intelligence*, and *Barron's* Big Money Poll as proof that there were few natural buyers of stocks left to propel a significant rally. In perhaps our best call at ISI last year, we disregarded the bearish signals we were receiving from these indicators, believing that they didn't fully capture the feelings of the hedge fund community.

While many speculators and mutual funds alike still view the hedge fund industry as a small and elite niche of investors, anecdotal evidence suggests that hedge funds represent between 35 and 40 percent of the Street's total commission budget, and by extension, at least that amount of the market's daily trading volume.[7] In essence, hedge funds are the market's most important marginal buyers and sellers of stock. As a result, it is dangerous to take the pulse of newsletter writers, institutional or retail investors, without also taking into account the sentiment of this new and crucial segment of the investment community.

At ISI, our Survey Group's hedge fund survey attempts to bridge this gap by measuring both net exposure (long minus short positions) and gross exposure (long plus short positions). In the absence of other indicators like our own, investors will likely be well served by looking at market-based indicators of sentiment like the CBOE Volatility Index and the put/call ratio.

Why Growth in the Industry Will Slow

Although most hedge fund managers would shudder at the thought, there are a number of reasons the hypergrowth in the industry is likely to slow. As we have seen, institutions and wealthy individuals are throwing money at these investment vehicles with little regard to a fund manager's track record or experience. And an alarming number of investment professionals are leaving relatively secure jobs at some successful and storied mutual fund complexes in the hope of attaining instant riches. But the fact that there are now actually more hedge funds than mutual funds in the United States should tell you something.

Very few industries double in size in three years without eventually experiencing some consolidation and rationalization. Historically, few good investments are made in industries with no barriers to entry. Regardless of the impressive résumés and confidence of this new breed of fund manager, there are a number of reasons why institutional investors and wealthy individuals are likely to slow their flow of funds into these highly speculative, and expensive, investment vehicles.

Performance

Perhaps the most compelling reason the growth in the hedge fund industry will slow is simply weak relative performance. While most in the industry will tell you that they provide stable "absolute" returns and are thus unconcerned with their performance relative to the major indices—like the S&P 500—the jury is still out as to whether their customers will feel comfortable paying 20 percent of the profits to a hedge fund for the privilege of underperforming the broader market.

To be sure, the accelerated growth in the industry came when the major indices showed massive losses in the 2000-02 period. And with the average hedge fund up 3 percent in 2002 despite a decline in the S&P 500 of greater than 20 percent, few investors cared about the 20 percent incentive fee. But as the market rallied in 2003 and many hedge funds were left behind, more investors started to wonder about the relative merits of paying outsized incentive fees. A continuation of the bull market will only heighten these concerns.

Regulatory and Competitive Blowback

The growth of hedge funds has hardly gone unnoticed, and it seems highly unlikely in the current environment that regulators and traditional money management firms aren't forming some sort of response. Financial shenanigans at brokerage firms and public companies have left regulators in a less than generous mood in their dealings with all financial institutions, and hedge funds will not be immune to this sentiment. In fact, the Treasury Department and the SEC have already indicated that greater oversight of hedge funds is in the works.

The responses from hedge funds' buy-side competition are more diffuse. While some mutual funds have already started their own hedge funds to retain talent, some responses being considered are more aggressive. In our travels around the country, we have heard rumblings among institutional investors about the wisdom of lending out their stocks for short sales, for which they have traditionally earned sizable fees.

At the depths of despair in the summer of 2002, I remember one of our customers at a mutual fund ask, "For 10 to 15 basis points, why on earth should I provide ammunition to the shorts that are killing our long positions every day?" To some the stuff of conspiracy theory, there are indications that such sentiments are gaining momentum.

In fact, in 2002 two large Dutch pension funds came under severe criticism for urging the world's 50 largest pension funds to curb their securities lending activities. It seems likely that such efforts will fall flat, but it does highlight concerns about the growth in alternative investment vehicles, if not anxiety on the part of some members of the traditional money management community. While there is no evidence that these sentiments are being acted upon, it is a trend worth watching. Long a significant source of profit for investment banks, a successful effort to curtail stock lending could also be a negative for broker/dealers.

Dividends Could Spell Trouble

There is also a chance that the new tax cut on dividends will slow the growth of the hedge fund industry. Because an investor shorting a stock owes the lender any dividend payments, the new tax law could, at the least, make shorting stocks more expensive, and at most greatly limit the number of shares available for stock loan.

It works like this. Before the administration's tax package was signed into law, it made no difference to investors whether they received their dividends directly from the company or from the person or entity to whom they lent their stock. The tax treatment for the directly received dividend (or the pass-through or "in lieu" dividend) would be the same—the investor's ordinary income rate. Under the new tax law, however, only dividends directly received from the company will be available for the lower tax rate. As a result, short sellers will need to compensate holders for the difference in the tax treatment of their shares. According to Lehman's Robert Willens, stock lenders will demand $1.30 for each dollar of dividend income forgone.

Retail investors and mutual funds may have a strong incentive to keep their shares in cash rather than margin accounts to avoid this level of complexity, potentially greatly diminishing the number of shares available to be sold short. While the IRS has indicated that it was going to give brokerage firms a pass on this issue in 2003, 2004 could be one of great upheaval for brokerage firms and short-sellers alike. Again, brokerage firms that specialize in stock loan and prime brokerage activities may be especially vulnerable.

The High Water Mark

Of course, I'm not the first person to suggest that a 1 percent management fee and a 20 percent incentive fee is excessive. Hedge fund managers rightfully point out that paying for performance aligns the interests of the client with the interests of the fund's general partner. They are also quick to point out the existence of the *high water mark*, a feature unique to money managed in hedge funds rather than mutual funds.

The high water mark clause in the offering memorandum typically requires the fund to achieve a minimum rate of return or to recoup any losses by new profits before it can claim its incentive fee. This is the main reason hedge funds are considered "absolute return vehicles": To earn their keep, they need to earn a profit regardless of the broader market's direction. Since mutual funds are managed without an incentive fee, they are typically considered "relative return vehicles."

In theory, the high water mark sounds great. Who wouldn't want to align the interests of their fund managers with their own financial interests? But there is a dark side of this practice to both the customer as well as the fund manager. As far as the customer is concerned, this form of remuneration might cause a fund manager to lock in gains made early in the year by avoiding calculated risks to secure his incentive fee. Far more dangerous is the perverse incentive given to the fund manager who shows losses to "gun" the performance of the fund by taking outsized risks in an effort to get paid. In either case, it is the size of the incentive fee that might cause the interests of the fund manager to supersede those of his clients.

While it seems clear that the high water mark can present risks to the limited partners of hedge funds, it also involves significant business risk to the fund manager himself. That is because, after a particularly difficult year, the hedge fund manager might face the prospect of "working for free" indefinitely, ruining the value of the concern he created. Consider the fact that a fund that is down 50 percent in any given year needs to be up 100 percent before it can receive any incentive fee. This risk is not insignificant and, as we will now see, could affect the most talented of fund managers.

Case Study: Tiger Management

Despite the superstar status afforded to hedge funds in the heady days of the 1960s, the bear markets in 1969–1970 and in 1973–1974 brought low the outsized expectations that these new structures and new fund managers could provide. The alternative investment industry largely returned to the relative obscurity it enjoyed in its embryonic stages, when only Alfred Jones and a few of his alumni ran "hedged" funds. But the spotlight was once again thrust onto hedge funds when the influential magazine *Institutional Investor* featured the remarkable performance of Julian Robertson and his Tiger Management Company in 1986.

Despite the enormous success it enjoyed for the better part of 20 years, perhaps the greatest example of the weaknesses of the hedge fund model (and especially the risk associated with the high water mark) was the rise and fall of Tiger Management, considered one the best investment funds of all time. In the purpose of full disclosure, my best friend in life and godfather to my son, Jay Coyle, worked as a trader for the illustrious fund for six years. Seeing Jay at his office was always a particular treat for me, for if the devil himself had an office suite in Manhattan, he might very well have envied Tiger's. The company attracted the best, the brightest, and, I might add, the nicest people on Wall Street.

A former broker and head of Kidder Peabody's investment advisory business, North Carolina native Julian Robertson turned the $8 million he started his fund with in 1980 into over $20 billion in 1998, posting an annualized return of 32 percent. Not surprisingly, this type of record and organization started to attract the attention of large financial institutions wishing to build assets and capitalize on the cashflow only a hedge fund could provide. In 1998 an article in *The Wall Street Journal* recounted discussions between Robertson and Goldman Sachs that valued the firm at nearly $6 billion.

And yet, 18 months later, Julian Robertson decided to liquidate all of the funds under the Tiger Management umbrella, essentially writing down the value of his firm to zero. How could the value of any organization, especially one with the talent and ethical standards of Tiger, change so quickly?

In retrospect it was quite simple: Robertson's long-term and studied approach to the market was at odds with the manic Internet boom of the late 1990s. Going long the world's best companies and shorting its worst ones, Tiger suffered such significant losses in 1999 and early

2000 that the analysts and portfolio managers needed to earn 48 percent in order to surpass the water mark and to once again charge incentive fees. This episode revealed the vagaries of the traditional hedge fund structure and was an object lesson to future fund managers for generations. The cruel irony in this whole affair was that Tiger's largest positions—US Air and United Asset Management—turned around in the months following Tiger's liquidation. Hedge fund managers and potential hedge fund investors alike should bear in mind that if it could happen to Julian Robertson, it could happen to anyone.

The Future: Past as Prologue?

If the go-go years and reports that George Soros broke the bank of England in 1992 weren't enough, the mystery, luster, and fear of the hedge fund structure was heightened further when a group of traders, with the help of a couple of Nobel laureates, brought the global financial markets to the brink of ruin through Long Term Capital Management. And thus one of the more interesting features of the history of the hedge fund industry is how the public and the media has at various times viewed them as the ultimate exemplification of free markets and at others as opportunistic cancers on the global financial system. Being a fan of free markets I am inclined to go with the former. But regardless of one's views on these investment vehicles, few can ignore their impact on today's financial markets.

Ultimately, the current love affair with hedge funds, and the risks involved in their operation, are not a whole lot different than they were a generation ago. Prior to the liquidation of his own investment partnership at the tail end of the go-go 1960s, despite a compound return of 25.3 percent over 11 years, Warren Buffett was quoted as saying: "We live in an investing world, populated not by those who must logically be persuaded to believe, but by the hopeful, credulous and greedy, grasping for an excuse to believe … I am not attuned to this market environment, and I don't want to spoil a decent record by trying to play a game I don't understand."

Nearly thirty years later, Julian Robertson wrote in his final letter to clients: "In an irrational market, where earnings and price considerations take a back seat to mouse clicks and momentum, [our] logic, as we have learned doesn't count for much…. What I do know is that there is no point in subjecting our investors to risk in a market which frankly we do not understand."

In the next several years, a number of questions about the growth of the industry will need to be answered. First and foremost, will institutions, which have been the biggest purchasers of hedge fund services, have the patience to pay 20 percent incentive fees when the industry invariably underperforms the broader market? While the flexibility that hedge funds provide may in fact warrant a higher fee structure, it also remains to be seen whether hedge funds will ever start to compete on price. Ultimately, the growth in the hedge fund structure may fall under its own weight. Of the nearly 8,000 total, in the final analysis there may be relatively few that can provide consistent above-market returns. In the meantime, short- and long-term investors alike should be aware of the uncommon influence these new investment vehicles are currently having on the business as a whole.

Key Take-Aways

1. Hedge funds can be broadly defined as lightly regulated limited partnerships that can employ a variety of different investment tools, including leverage and short sales, trade in a variety of different financial products, and can charge an incentive fee for their services.
2. The assets in hedge funds may be small in comparison to their mutual fund cousins, but the fact that they account for 35 to 40 percent of the Wall Street commissions make their influence significant.
3. Hedge funds have increased volumes, increased the demand for talented investment professionals, made sell-side research less dependent on valuation, and increased the popularity of performance fees.
4. The high water mark and outsized performance fees represent risks for the ongoing concern value of hedge funds and for investors.
5. Increased regulation, lackluster performance from new entrants, and increased dividend payouts may all slow the pace of the growth in the hedge fund industry.

3

WASHINGTON BECOMES THE CENTER OF THE UNIVERSE

HOW 9/11 AND CORPORATE SCANDALS HAVE SHIFTED THE BALANCE OF INVESTMENT POWER

"We make progress at night—while the politicians sleep."
—BRAZILIAN PROVERB

WHILE IT MIGHT BE DIFFICULT for any native New Yorker to imagine, it seems likely that Washington's impact on Wall Street will be more important in the years to come than in any other period in the history of America's financial markets. The pendulum between Pennsylvania Avenue and Wall Street has swung from total indifference (1920s and 1950s) to alarming proximity (1930s and 1970s) and has long been the subject of market soors and journalists alike. But the current collision course between these two spheres of influence was to a large degree set by the attack on the World Trade Center on September 11, 2001, and the revelations about corporate malfeasance in the summer of 2002. There is, of course, no moral equivalency between these two events, but their impact on the nation's psyche was much the same: Increasingly, Americans have called on the federal government to provide greater protections for their economic and physical security.

I know of no one who has worked on Wall Street for any length of time who wasn't profoundly affected by the horrific attack on 9/11. In the course of 18 minutes, terrorists changed the way Americans and Wall Street viewed the role of the federal government. That these attacks came after the end of the great boom on Wall Street of the late 1990s may have been seen by some as a sign from Providence that the heady days of the bubble were over. Indeed, less than a year later, shareholders would also be forced to come to grips with the realization that all was not as it seemed in corporate America, and that in many respects the companies to which they entrusted their hard-earned savings had failed them. Here too investors had to wonder about the role of public institutions, like the SEC, in securing fair markets.

The bad news didn't stop there. The events of 9/11 in 2001 and the corporate scandals that shook America's view of itself in 2002 were only heightened by the war on Iraq and the public scandals involving the New York Stock Exchange and the mutual fund industry in 2003. Fortunately, by then the strength in stocks suggested that investors were once again confident that the nation was taking steps to ensure greater protections from terrorism and from corporate abuses. But this new-found confidence has come with certain costs. As the decline in the role of the federal government in our nation's economy paved the way for an expansion of earnings multiples in the '80s and '90s, the growing role of government may indeed result in larger deficits, higher long-term interest rates, and lower stock market returns in the years to come.

While many on Wall Street at least try to feign some sort of benign indifference to what goes on inside the Beltway, there are a few firms that see the potentially enormous impact of legislation and politics on the performance of the economy, financial markets, and individual stocks. Tom Gallagher and Andy Laperriere head our Washington office at ISI, and their work has greatly aided my own research and investment strategy. In the first half of this chapter we will explore the historical impact of war and exogenous shocks to stock market returns as a basis for understanding how our involvement in Iraq will shape the investment landscape in the next decade. In the second half we will explore the limits and opportunities of government power and presidential politics in influencing the economy and the financial markets.

War and Market Performance

There is perhaps no event that is currently shaping the political process and the limits and opportunities of America's power like the war on terrorism and our efforts to create a democratic state in Iraq. The $87.5 billion package the President secured in the fall of 2003 to rebuild Iraq and to prosecute the war on terrorism appears, sadly, to be only the beginning of a long struggle.

While it's hard to imagine that the daily headlines from Iraq don't have a meaningful and deleterious impact on the markets and the economy, the historical record indicates that the impact of war on market performance is not as clear as one might expect. Indeed, as Table 3-1 indicates, the market performed relatively well during World War II, the Korean War, and the first Gulf war, but languished during the Vietnam years. That conflict, along with a significant increase in government spending associated with the Great Society, produced lackluster returns for the market from 1964 to 1975.

TABLE 3-1   Military Conflicts and Market Returns

Conflict	Start and End Dates	Event	S&P 500
World War II	December 7, 1941	Pearl Harbor	9.3
	August 14, 1945	V-J Day	14.7
		% Change	**57.7%**
		Average Annual % Change	**15.7%**
Korean War	June 25, 1950	N. Korea Invades S. Korea	19.1
	July 25, 1953	Truce Signed	24.2
		% Change	**26.6%**
		Average Annual % Change	**8.6%**
Vietnam Conflict	August 7, 1964	Gulf of Tonkin Resolution Signed	81.9
	April 30, 1975	Fall of Saigon	87.3
		% Change	**6.6%**
		Average Annual % Change	**0.6%**
Gulf War	August 2, 1990	Iraq Invades Kuwait	351.5
	April 6, 1991	Cease-fire Accepted	375.4
		% Change	**6.79%**
		Average Annual % Change	**10.0%**

So far, the market has largely shrugged off the risks associated with the second Gulf war, but the longer our involvement in Iraq and the greater the costs associated with it, the harder it will be for stocks to make progress. The obvious conclusion is that the market performs well during relatively "short" wars where we are successful and poorly during long and drawn-out campaigns where our success is more uncertain. Given these findings, the present course of our involvement in Iraq suggests that investors could be in for a tough time in the next few years. But as we are about to see, where there is risk, there is always opportunity.

Market Performance and Exogenous Shocks

The specter of 9/11 has forced both policy makers and investors to try to consider the unthinkable. Since that terrible day, there have been very few meetings in which one of our firm's clients hasn't asked me how another exogenous shock or major terrorist act on U.S. soil would affect our firm's proposed investment strategy. It's an almost impossible question to answer, of course, for who knows where and when terrorists might strike again?

Avoiding investments in common stocks and other financial assets altogether is inappropriate, given the magnitude of America's response to this new world of multivariate threats. And yet, it also seems inappropriate to totally ignore the danger of another significant terrorist act. Personally, I am of the belief that America is now safer than it has been in some time, if merely because it is more aware of the threats facing it. But it seems clear that the cost of equity capital will be somewhat higher in an environment in which another 9/11 is possible, albeit unlikely.

Although there are few historical precedents for the dangerous new world of terrorism, studying market performance after four other shocks to the global political order—the attack on Pearl Harbor, the Cuban Missile Crisis, the assassination of President Kennedy, and the Iraqi invasion of Kuwait—suggests that the market seems to make a clear distinction between events that appear to introduce new and systemic risk, like Pearl Harbor and 9/11, and those that seem isolated and of relatively shorter duration, like the Cuban Missile Crisis and the assassination of President Kennedy.

Pearl Harbor, the Cuban Missile Crisis, and the Kennedy Assassination

To start with the Sunday attack on Pearl Harbor, it's safe to say that the market had already pretty much discounted war by the time the attack happened. On Monday, December 8, 1941, the market was down 2.9 percent, and it was down by as much as 8 percent at one point in the weeks following Pearl Harbor. The market did rally toward the end of December, but was down sharply in the spring of 1942 after a series of Axis victories. The market only bested its pre–Pearl Harbor level when it became clearer that the Allies would ultimately prove victorious in early 1943.

Although it is difficult for anyone under 50 years of age to imagine, the world seemed as if it were on the precipice of nuclear war in October 1962, when the Soviet Union decided to install nuclear weapons on the island of Cuba, only 90 miles off the coast of Florida. But while the market fell by as much as 5 percent from its precrisis high after President Kennedy's address to the nation during the Cuban Missile Crisis, it quickly dusted itself off when the crisis ended peacefully. It is interesting to note that the month following this dangerous standoff, November 1962, was, incidentally, the Dow's best month since September 1939.

Similarly, the market fell 2.9 percent on the day President Kennedy was assassinated—Friday, November 22, 1963—and, while the market was closed on the following Monday, it rallied on Tuesday, after it seemed apparent that President Johnson was firmly in control of the nation. The Dow actually went on to hit a record high within weeks of the assassination.

Not surprising, given the brutality of the attack on 9/11, the severity of the sell-off in the days after that fateful day put U.S. financial markets into uncharted territory. But this quick study of market performance after other exogenous shocks to the world political order should give investors confidence that the markets are extremely efficient in discounting the long-lasting impact of such events on the economy.

Determining Geopolitical Risk: The Importance of Oil

It's ironic, given the quantity of information available from the government and through the media, that investors can rely on few concrete indicators to determine when the threat of terrorism and geopolitical risk is high enough to warrant greater caution in their portfolios.

One potential method for determining the likelihood of imminent terrorist acts would be to monitor the Department of Homeland

Security's Terror Advisory System. Developed in the aftermath of 9/11 to give individuals, the public, and private institutions the government's assessment of the likelihood of an imminent terrorist attack, status changes appear to have had at least a short-term impact on the market. In the fall of 2002, for instance, the day after a downgrade in the terror advisory level from "High" to "Elevated" led to a 4 percent rally in the S&P (see Chart 3-1).

But while it seems clear that investors do indeed pay attention to this system and invest accordingly, its brief history and infrequent status changes have made it an imperfect tool for investors wishing to monitor the ebbs and flows of America's war on terrorism.

Given what I do for a living, I'm obviously biased, but I believe the markets themselves—because they reflect all available information of market participants rather than the opinions of a select few—are the best leading indicators for changes in the economy and, to a degree, changes in the domestic and international political system as well. In this regard, the price of oil, given its intimate relationship with a part of world that has recently been a source of much animosity toward the United States, is perhaps the single best indicator of potential terrorist acts and geopolitical tensions.

Oil's reputation as an important leading indicator for both economic growth and global political tensions has grown substantially since the 1970s. Perhaps the best example of black gold's predictive powers came in 1990–1991. As recounted in CNBC anchor Ron Insana's book, *The Message of the Markets,* oil prices started sending loud signals of impending trouble in the spring and summer of 1990, long before Iraq

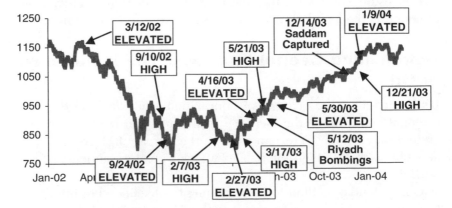

CHART 3-1   S&P 500 and Terror Advisory Levels

invaded Kuwait and Saddam Hussein captured the national conscious-
ness. While the price of oil had remained relatively stable since 1986,
prices started to rise swiftly in June 1990, correctly anticipating a cut in
oil production in July and, ultimately, new tensions in the Middle East.

Although many felt that Iraq in 1990 was unlikely to pose a threat
to its neighbors given its long and bloody war with Iran in the 1980s,
oil market participants who heard rumblings that Iraqi troops were
amassing on the Kuwaiti border began to bid up the price of oil. The
price rose from $15 a barrel in early June to nearly $30 by the time
Iraq invaded Kuwait on August 2, 1990. Oil prices would eventually
top $40 by October, when uncertainty surrounding the world's
response reached its zenith (see Chart 3-2). But in much the same way
that the increase correctly anticipated growing geopolitical tensions,
the price decline correctly forecast the Allied victory over Iraq and the
securing of Kuwaiti oilfields.[1]

While it seems clear that investors should have an intense interest
and respect for the information the price of crude oil provides about
the international political sphere, it is also difficult to overestimate the
impact of changes in energy prices on economic growth. As a matter
of fact, there are only two inputs into ISI's most basic GDP model:
changes in G7 short rates, and changes in the price of oil.

Given the fact that the United States consumes roughly 7 billion barrels of crude oil each year, a simple, back-of-the-envelope calculation
suggests that every dollar decline in the price of oil frees up $7 billion
in liquidity annually. In this context, a good case can be made that low
and stable oil prices were a major contributor to the boom in the 1990s,
while higher energy prices have been a significant factor in the market's
woes in the last few years. As a matter of fact, the average price of crude

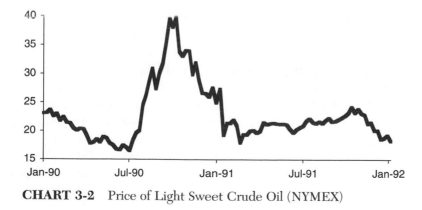

CHART 3-2   Price of Light Sweet Crude Oil (NYMEX)

oil was $19 from the start of the recovery in March 1991 through the remainder of the decade. Since January 2000, in contrast, the price of oil has averaged over $28—clearly a major headwind for the economy and the market.

There are obvious limits to an administration's ability to lower energy prices, but at the margin, President Bush has an enormous political incentive to see lower oil prices before the 2004 election. Despite some of the gloomier headlines, Iraq's oil production has increased substantially since the invasion and at one point exceeded prewar levels of 2.5 million barrels a day. Investors will be well served to pay attention to oil, a great leading economic indicator and, increasingly, a good indicator of geopolitical tensions. Time will tell if the Bush Administration's grand plans for Iraq will be realized.

Investment Opportunities in the Defense Sector

At the height of the cold war, the U.S. military was structured to fight a two-front war against both conventional and nuclear forces. But with the break-up of the Soviet Union and the emergence of Russia and new sovereign states, the Department of Defense has had to adapt to fight an enemy, to use the vernacular of the military, of "many faces in many places."

No longer protected by distance or the oceans, the United States currently faces the threat of rogue nations, like North Korea, and non-state entities, like al Qaeda. In many respects, America's conventional and nuclear dominance has forced its enemies to rely on acts of terrorism to achieve their aims. The emergence of this new threat to U.S. security is forcing the Defense Department to retool the country's military apparatus, changing the course our military will need to take to fight the war on terrorism. This new approach should result in greater defense research, development, and investment.

Of course, a significant potential fly in the ointment with the secular case for defense spending is that the country's growing budget deficit may force policy makers to turn off the procurement spigot. But, as Chart 3-3 on the following page indicates, defense spending as a percentage of GDP has fallen from about 14 percent in the early 1950s to about 4 percent today. While that may not be surprising in an environment where technology rather than personnel is being used to boost military effectiveness and productivity, there may be some sense that defense cuts have gone too far and that an increase in the procurement budget is necessary.

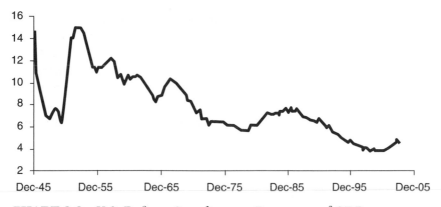

CHART 3-3 U.S. Defense Spending as a Percentage of GDP

Andy Laperriere of our Washington team has noted that the Congressional Budget Office estimates that the Pentagon will need to spend between $111 and $130 billion on a steady-state basis to maintain the country's force readiness. Given the fact that the United States spent only $70 billion in 2003, the potential impact on the budget deficit and the country's procurement budget is enormous. The costs associated with the war on terror and their concomitant impact on the country's force structure makes it tempting to sell government bonds and buy defense contractors for the long term.

Remarkable but perhaps not surprising to those living in Southern California or on Long Island, the number of prime contractors to the Pentagon has fallen to only five.[2] While there are hundreds if not thousands of smaller contractors in the defense industry, they are often too small and lack the access to the capital markets that is necessary for meaningful research and development. This is crucial in an era where the military is becoming more reliant on technology than personnel.

In my travels to Europe and Asia, investors often ask me about the U.S. defense industry. With relatively few natural investment opportunities in defense outside the United States, American and foreign investors have few choices when wishing to play the industry. Greater demand for defense shares, and a limited supply, also suggests that U.S. defense stocks might outperform the broader market in the years to come.

The wide-ranging threats facing America and free nations everywhere is leading to changes in the defense spending of other countries as well. In "Cautiously, Japan Returns to Combat in Southern Iraq," the *Wall Street Journal* recently highlighted how greater pressure from the United States to provide for its own defense, growing tensions with North Korea, and the desire to check China's growing military influence has contributed to a growing desire within Japan to amend its constitution and abandon its five-decade policy of defense-only security forces.[3] Recently, Japan's decision to place troops in Iraq marked its most significant and controversial military deployment since World War II. To the extent to which Japan remains among the world's largest economies, this appears to represent a seismic shift in the amount of global resources devoted to military expenditures. It seems likely that other countries are contemplating similar moves. Like it or not, the perception that the world is becoming more dangerous means that defense spending is likely to rise not only in the United States, but also around the world.

In an environment of limited multiple expansion and lower and more stable returns, investors should seek industries with natural tailwinds of increases in aggregate demand. Even if one is a true believer in the cyclical recovery, we believe it's important to have stocks in the portfolio that effectively hedge against a more uncertain world in the aftermath of 9/11. In this regard, defense stocks may be the best defense.

Investing in Iraq's Reconstruction Efforts

Unfortunately, the fractious nature of Iraq's internal politics and the threats posed by nonstate terrorist entities make it appear that the United States will be in Iraq for a while. If there is any silver lining in this dark cloud, it may be that U.S. companies will be among the most visible in the effort to rebuild, modernize, and expand Iraq's infrastructure and oil industry. The country's oil reserves (estimated at 110 billion barrels) stand as its most valuable asset, and will, of course, require the greatest capital investment.

The Iraqi oil industry has suffered greatly from neglect and mismanagement since the Iran-Iraq War in the 1980s. According to some estimates, bringing its oil fields back to their pre-1991 production of 3.5 million barrels per day could cost as much as $5 billion. Oil and gas equipment and services companies such as Halliburton, Baker-Hughes, and Schlumberger all appear to be in-country for the long haul.

Economic mismanagement and the war also require large investments in Iraqi's commercial and public buildings, housing, medical facilities, and land, sea, and air transportation infrastructure. As a result, multinational engineering and construction firms like Flour,

Bechtel, and Perini Construction, as well capital goods producers like Caterpillar and Ingersoll Rand, appear to be likely beneficiaries.

But the benefits to American business go far beyond capital goods companies. Both air freight and container shipping concerns should be able to capitalize on the necessary shipments of military and construction matériel. Tanker companies will likely see greater demand for their services transporting oil and natural gas from the region. In today's environment of technology-heavy engineering, even tech companies—specifically those in the computer hardware industry—may see an increase in demand for computers and communication hardware from construction firms headed to the Gulf. Anecdotally, these businesses have done well supplying large domestic capital projects like Boston's Big Dig and Salt Lake City's preparation for the Olympic Games. Further, industrial machinery companies and makers of self-powered generators such as American Power Conversion and GE may see a pickup in orders.[4]

The '62 Market Drop: Kennedy vs. U.S. Steel

Of course, the government's ability to influence the financial markets goes far beyond its military and diplomatic efforts. If investors had any doubt about the potential impact of domestic policies on stock prices, they were largely put to rest in 1962, when a bitter confrontation between President Kennedy and U.S. Steel resulted in a market correction that would ultimately erase 57 percent of the market's 1957–1961 advance.

Although an increasingly activist SEC, a burgeoning scandal at the American Stock Exchange, and growing anxieties about U.S. involvement in Vietnam were all concerns at the start of 1962, it appeared that most investors maintained an uneasy peace with lofty stock prices. Despite the extraordinarily high valuations afforded to bellwethers such as IBM and Polaroid (80 and 100 times earnings, respectively), the market was largely flat in the first several months of the year. But the eerie calm was shattered in April when President Kennedy faced off against the president of U.S. Steel, Roger Blough, precipitating a 27 percent drop in the Dow Industrials in little more than a month, and culminating, on May 28, in the largest single-day point loss since 1929.

Intimately involved in the intense wage negotiations between big steel and its unions, President Kennedy had worked hard to ensure a fair settlement for months, putting pressure on the unions to moderate their wage demands and on the steel industry to hold the line on prices. He was pleased and relieved when the ultimate agreement, which involved no general wage hike and no price increases, was signed on March 31. But Kennedy's political victory was short-lived, and his pleasure at the ultimate settlement quickly turned to anger when U.S. Steel, in a shocking move, announced a $6 per ton increase in the price of steel less than two weeks after the labor contract was signed.[5] In an effort to stem the tide in a five-year slide in earnings, other major steel companies, like Bethlehem Steel, Republic, Jones & Laughlin, Youngstown, and Wheeling, followed suit. Of the 12 major steel companies in the country, all but five decided to join U.S. Steel and raise prices, representing 83 percent of total industry capacity.

President Kennedy felt betrayed and viewed U.S. Steel's decision as an affront to the office of the presidency and a potential threat to the national economy. While there is broad disagreement among historians about the scope of his administration's efforts in the ensuing weeks, there is little doubt that the President vigorously sought to roll back the price increases. By all accounts, the administration brought the full force of the government to bear to persuade those joining and not join-ing U.S. Steel's price hike. Offhanded comments from Bethlehem Steel president Edmund Martin the day after Blough announced his decision became the basis for a Federal Trade Commission investiga-tion into whether the action violated a 1951 consent decree. A Department of Justice investigation ensued. The Department of Defense got into the act, awarding a major contract for the Polaris sub-marine to Lukens Steel, a company that had held the line on pricing. After great drama, U.S. Steel rescinded its price increases less than 72 hours after it informed the President of its initial decision.[6]

But while the President rolled the dice and won, his victory came at a very high price as far as the markets were concerned. Although it was the subject of some doubt, Kennedy was widely reported as say-ing, "My father always told me that all businessmen were sons of bitches, but I never believed it till now."

On top of all this, the SEC was investigating everything from insider trading to unregistered stock sales, further souring the mood on Wall Street. Ultimately, investors viewed the administration as antibusiness, a moniker that's about as effective as Kryptonite in stop-ping broad advances in stocks. By April 1962 the Kennedy panic started in earnest, continuing unabated through March 1963 and leav-ing the Dow Industrials 22 percent lower in the process (see Chart 3-4). U.S. Steel dropped from 91 to 38.

CHART 3-4 1962 S&P 500 Market Decline

Although the economy was strong enough to withstand the broad sell-off in stocks through June, it imparted a significant lesson to market historians and investors alike: What happens in Washington can have an enormous impact on the behavior of the financial markets. Although there have been few showdowns between an administration and Big Business in the years since, the Clinton administration's antitrust lawsuit against one of the country's most successful and efficient companies, Microsoft, has sometimes been cited as a meaningful talisman of growing government power at the expense of Big Business at the tail end of the bubble years.

Regulators Gain the Upper Hand

While Kennedy's 1962 incursion into Big Business was jarring to investors, the increased importance and power of regulators was welcomed by scores of retail investors, and even some institutional investors, in the post-1990s bubble years. By the fall of 2003 most institutional investors and any regular watcher of the nightly news couldn't help but become familiar with New York Attorney General Eliot Spitzer. The historic fines imposed on Wall Street's most powerful investment banks over their research practices, the stiff sentences handed down to wayward corporate chieftains, and the massive reforms taking place at the New York Stock Exchange all point to the increased power and influence of government over the financial markets.

Remarkably, this is nothing new to Wall Street. The pendulum of regulatory oversight often swings from indifference in boom years to intense scrutiny once the party has ended. The Pecora Commission hearings in Congress into Wall Street practices in the aftermath of the 1929 crash, for example, led to the creation of the Securities and Exchange Commission and Glass-Steagal legislation. While the amplitude of these swings appears to be growing, one would presume and hope that this influence will wane with the passage of time.

Meanwhile, Wall Street is making huge efforts to stay on the right side of today's new regulatory regime. In Chapter 4, we will explore in greater detail ways in which investors might be able to capitalize on new reform legislation such as Sarbanes-Oxley and Regulation G.

The Limits of Government Influence: The Go-Go Years

While Wall Street should be chastened in the belief that it will never be able escape the long arm of regulation, the federal government should also realize the limits of its power over Wall Street. Although Kennedy's showdown with U.S. Steel and President Bush's tax cuts are important examples of the potential power of political developments on the investment process, it is important to note that government actions alone are not enough to fully and immediately overcome dislocations in the economy and excessive valuations in stocks. This was never more evident than in the period of reform following the so-called go-go market in the late 1960s.

While rising inflation and interest rates make the 1968–1970 market decline an imperfect parallel with the drop in 2000–2003, unprecedented public participation in the market, a marked rise in the influence of hedge funds, shaky accounting practices, and the rise of conglomerates (à la Tyco in the 1990s) make the bear market that ended the go-go years eerily similar to the end of the bubble experienced at the tail end of the Internet boom.

Widespread social anxieties also make the 1968–1970 market decline a natural choice for aspiring market historians. An uneasy Republican administration was in power at the time, trying to provide some solace to a population beset by a combination of record trade and budget deficits, the invasion of Cambodia, and the Kent State tragedy. The more activist role of the administration and the SEC under Bill Donaldson taken in recent years to restore investor confidence is also reminiscent of the go-go period.

But President Bush should remember that while governments can level the playing field for investors, they have little influence, in the short term, on prices in a free market. President Nixon's attempts to halt the slide in stocks in 1970 should serve as a useful reminder to everyone in the administration about the limits of government power.

In an effort to convince the investing public that it was not oblivious to the destruction of wealth that accompanied the end of one of the most speculative periods in U.S. history, President Nixon, at the urging of longtime friend, NYSE Chairman Bunny Lasker, hosted a dinner at the White House comprised of 60 leading figures from business and finance. Remarkably, news of the administration's newfound interest in the stock market, along with some soothing words from the Fed, led to the largest single point gain in the Dow in history up to that time.

President Bush should take little comfort in this episode, however, as revelations of the Penn Central bankruptcy brought about a new round of selling in June 1970. Ultimately, fancy footwork on the part of the Fed averted a widespread financial calamity in the wake of Penn Central, and the Dow began a long and fairly steady march by year's end.

The Presidential Election Cycle

Perhaps another indication of the impact Washington can have on the financial markets is the much talked about presidential election cycle. Yale Hirsch, former *Barron's* columnist and author of the respected annual *Stock Trader's Almanac*, popularized the strong relationship between stock market returns and the quadrennial presidential election. Hirsch noticed that bear markets have typically occurred in the first and second years of a President's term, while the third and fourth years have been kind for the performance of the stocks. Many have speculated that this occurs because Presidents tend to make tough decisions about the economy immediately following their election, and gradually propose economy and market-friendly legislation as the next election draws closer.

While the presidential election cycle is probably not enough to overcome more important considerations like valuations and interest rates when deciding to invest, the empirical data does suggest that Hirsch's observations are statistically significant. Since 1928, the total return on the S&P averaged 7.5 percent in the first year of a President's term, 8.1 percent in the second year, 18.7 percent in the third, and 13.6 percent in the fourth. The market's strength in the third and fourth years appears to be statistically significant in a period in which the average total return has been +12.2 percent (see Chart 3-5).

When I talk about this phenomenon in presentations, I am invariably asked, "Does the market prefer Republican or Democrat administrations?" While stocks have shown little preference for either party controlling the White House, the market has performed better during Democratic administrations. The presidential election cycle has been even more pronounced when one excludes the Great Crash of the Hoover Administration. Since 1945, the market has been up 21.9 and 14.0 percent in the third and fourth years of Democrat administrations, and up 21.9 and 11.5 percent during Republican administrations.

Tort Reform

In addition to the growing power of government, investors have increasingly been forced to pay attention to another, and more insidious, assault on business through public institutions. It doesn't require a lot of courage to hold this view, but the growing influence of trial lawyers on the political process and on the economy should be a concern for all investors. Brian Olson, senior fellow at the Manhattan Institute, has claimed that trial lawyers have become the fourth branch of government, supplanting the traditional roles of elected officials and regulators. A 2002 decision by a California jury to award a tobacco

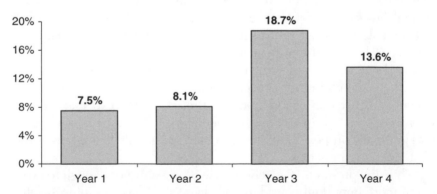

CHART 3-5 Presidential Election Cycle. Average S&P Returns by Year of Term Since 1928

plaintiff $28 billion highlights some of the absurdities inherent in our current ability and penchant to sue (and possibly win) in America.

Although I had some vague sense of the costs associated with the growth in class action lawsuits, I had no idea of the scope of the potential problem until I read a new paper on the subject from the Manhattan Institute, "Trial Lawyers Inc." Highlighting the "industry's" growth, the study reported a threefold increase in federal class action suits and a tenfold increase in state class action suits against U.S. corporations. It also claimed that asbestos litigation in and of itself has forced 67 companies to declare bankruptcy, many of which have never manufactured or installed asbestos. Perhaps even more disturbing, the study found that less than half of the settlements actually go to the actual plaintiffs, with less than a quarter used to compensate victims for their economic damages.[7] (See Table 3-2.)

Lest one think this is only a problem for "Smokestack America," there are indications that the recent drama in our own industry might make financial services companies the final leg in a class action trifecta for the trial lawyers after tobacco and asbestos. The growth in class action suits is important for investors, and tort reform could be a powerful antidote against the limited prospects for multiple expansion in the years to come.

The importance of a new secular change for the U.S. economy is important for longer-term stock returns. That's because interest rates are already so low that it seems likely that stock market returns will be more in line with nominal GDP growth and corporate profits for the next several years. In retrospect, the slow and steady decline in both short- and long-term interest rates has been an enormous tailwind for higher earnings multiples and, by extension, stock market performance in the 1980s and 1990s.

While the President's tax cut on dividends and capital gains in 2003 was a seminal event for stocks that should warrant a higher than average multiple, already lower levels of interest rates make it difficult to foresee higher earnings multiples without another significant structural change in the economy.

Further tax reform, a greater commitment to free trade, and the capture of Osama bin Laden would all be welcome developments for investors in common stocks, but no other change would boost business and investor confidence more quickly and dramatically than tort reform. This is, of course, easier said than done. The same Manhattan Institute study claimed that trial lawyers have contributed over $470 million in federal campaign contributions since 1990.[8]

TABLE 3-2   2000–2002 Asbestos Related Bankruptcies

A-Best

AC&S

A.P. Green Industries

Armstrong World Indsutries

ASARTRA (Synkoloid)

Babcock & Wilcox

Bethlehem Steel

Burns & Roe Enterprises

Eastco Industrial Safety

E.J. Bartels

Federal Mogul

G-I Holdings

Harbison-Walker

J.T. Thorpe

Kaiser Aluminum

MacArthur Companies

North American Refractory

Owens Corning

Pittsburgh Corning

Pilbrico

Porter Hayden

Shook & Fletcher

Skinner Engine

Swan Transportatiom

USG Corporatiom

Washington Group International

W.R. Grace

Our Washington team believes that while the prospects for tort reform are improving in more states, it has not reached critical mass in Washington. Andy Laperriere notes that the Democrats in Congress have blocked every tort reform effort, from medical malpractice to asbestos to class action reform. But there is reason for hope. It appears that tort reform will be a big issue in the 2004 campaign, and if the Democrats conclude that they paid a price for the issue in the election, and the GOP gains Senate seats, there is a chance we can look forward to reform in 2005 or 2006.

This may be an uphill battle, but businessmen and investors should keep in mind the potentially damaging effects the growth in this "industry" is having on the economy and, potentially, the market.

The Importance of the 2004 Election

When analyzing the potential impact of political changes on the stock market, good Wall Street analysts subjugate their own personal sentiments of what they want to happen and instead focus on what will happen. Religion and politics are often dangerous subjects to discuss with clients, but as we have seen thus far, a thorough understanding of potential changes in the political landscape can have a significant impact on stock market performance.

As the 2004 presidential election approaches, it seems clear that the stock market would prefer to see President Bush reelected and views a victory of Democratic challenger Kerry with fear and loathing. Why? It simply has to do with whether the market will view the tax cuts on capital gains and dividends as permanent (a Bush victory) or as temporary (a Kerry victory). Without making value judgments on all the other issues likely to influence voters at the polls this November, I firmly believe that stocks will sell off if investors get any sense that the hard-won tax cuts on equity investments would be overturned.

The President has stated time and again that he would like to extend the tax cuts on dividends and capital gains, making them permanent. The Democratic challenger, Massachusetts Senator Kerry, on the other hand, has made it clear that the tax cuts legislated over the last four years will be subject to change. Whether a Kerry administration would ultimately be able to pull this off is unclear and irrelevant—a Kerry victory would send an unfriendly message to Big Business and equity investors alike. Given the retail investors' experiences in the postbubble years, the Bush tax cuts were extremely important in restoring investor interest in equities and were a major contributor to the market's healthy gains in 2003. Any sign that the after-tax return on stock investments will diminish would be a major headwind for further market gains in the years to come.

The Future

The success or failure of the United States in Iraq, the growing importance of national security, and the increasing influence of government regulation on Wall Street mean that Washington will be a greater consideration in the investment process and, by extension, in the economy. This is likely to have major implications for investors making stock, sector, and asset allocation decisions. It seems likely that government spending will consume a greater percentage of GDP and that the cost of doing business in the United States will be higher without new structural changes, like tort reform. As a result, a sustained rally in stocks will be dependent upon political, military, and diplomatic successes that increase our society's sense of security.

Key Take-Aways

1. The events of 9/11 in 2001 and the corporate scandals of the last few years mean that Washington will likely have an outsized influence on the investment process in the next couple of years.
2. Stocks perform well during relatively "short" wars where the United States is successful, and poorly during long and drawn out campaigns where success is less certain.
3. Oil may be the best "leading indicator" of growing geopolitical tensions during the war on terror.
4. In the wake of the corporate scandals and the passage of Sarbanes-Oxley, regulators clearly have the upper hand on today's new Wall Street.
5. There is a discernible presidential election cycle in the United States—the third and fourth years of a President's term are the most beneficial for stock returns.
6. The courts will be a new front on the impact of politics on the financial markets.
7. The 2004 presidential election will be important for stock investors—any sense that the tax cuts on dividends and capital gains will be reversed will hurt stocks.

4

INVESTING IN GOOD
CORPORATE GOVERNANCE

PICKING COMPANIES THAT SHOW
SHAREHOLDERS RESPECT

"In case of doubt, decide in favor of what is correct."
—KARL KRAUS

T HE FOLLOWING EXCHANGE between legendary financier J. P. Morgan and the famed Pujo Committee investigating big money trusts in 1912 underscores how central the question of character was, and still is, when it comes to the subject of money and credit:

"Is not commercial credit based primarily upon money or property?"
"No sir; the first thing is character."
"Before money or property?"
"Before money or property or anything else. Money cannot buy it ... because a man I do not trust could not get money from me on all the bonds in Christendom."

Anyone who lived through the tumultuous big market declines and revelations about corporate malfeasance in the summer of 2002 on Wall Street will tell you that there were many times when it seemed as if our industry would be regulated into oblivion at best and, at worst, that our capitalistic system would take a generation to fully recover from the body blows of scandal. Time and again corporate

America was forced to take a hard look at itself and ask how an economic system founded on the rule of law could be home to such egregious acts of corporate mismanagement and criminality as seen at Enron, Tyco, and Worldcom.

Like it or not, economic freedom almost necessarily leaves investors open to the potential for scandal. That's the bad news. The good news is that history has taught us time and again that a democratic system with free markets can reform itself very quickly. In this chapter we will examine the boom-bust cycle of reform that has been the hallmark of our financial markets for the last century, discuss the broader implications of new landmark legislation like Sarbanes-Oxley, and finally offer a few simple methods by which individual investors can determine whether the companies in which they are interested actually have the best interests of shareholders at heart.

A Short History of Financial Skulduggery

As recounted by Edwin Lefevre in the investing classic *Reminiscences of a Stock Operator*, legendary speculator Jesse Livermore once said, "Another lesson I learned early is that there is nothing new in Wall Street. There can't be because speculation is as old as the hills. Whatever happens in the stock market today has happened before and will happen again."[1]

Although it may be hard to believe, given the drama in corporate America over the last few years, U.S. financial history has seen more than one cycle in which corporations, regulators, and investors failed in their roles as fiduciaries during periods of excessive speculation. As a matter of fact, the more one reads about the history of the financial markets, the easier it is to believe that we're all just reproducing the same epic motion picture with different actors and more modern financial instruments.

The growing power of the industrial and money trusts early in the twentieth century, for instance, which led Teddy Roosevelt's administration to seek the divestiture of Rockefeller's vaunted Standard Oil in 1911, was not unlike the public's demand for accountability from corporate chieftains in the wake of the Enron scandal in 2002. The Supreme Court's decision back then to break up the company, establishing the forerunners of Exxon, Mobil, Texaco, and Chevron, gave the little-known Congressman Arsene Pujo all the ammunition he needed to call for congressional hearings to look into J. P. Morgan's dealings the following year.[2]

Unfortunately, genuine outrage about financial skulduggery during boom years has been known to elicit political grandstanding after a bubble has burst, and can result in what some would consider excessive regulation. At such times, policymakers conclude that Wall Street and corporate America are incapable of policing themselves. While arguments abound as to whether it's right or necessary for government to break up companies that have too much power, one thing is certain: Politicians rarely hesitate to bring about reform in the wake of speculative episodes when the public at large has been harmed. John Kenneth Galbraith spoke about this phenomenon in his *Short History of Financial Euphoria*:

> **The final and common feature of the speculative episode—in stock markets, real estate, or junk bonds—is what happens after the inevitable crash. This, invariably, will be a time of anger and recrimination and also of profoundly unsubtle introspection. The anger will fix upon the individuals who were previously most admired for their financial imagination and acuity. Some of them, having been persuaded of their own exemption from confining orthodoxy, will, as noted, have gone beyond the law, and their fall, and, occasionally, their incarceration, will now be viewed with righteous satisfaction.**[3]

Those who think New York Attorney General Eliot Spitzer is a thoroughly modern product of his times should consider the tactics of legal counsel Ferdinand Pecora when Congress led investigations into Wall Street in the aftermath of the crash of 1929. The Wall Street executives called before his committee were so unwilling to cooperate that Pecora often resorted to Barnumlike feats of showmanship to embarrass and cajole big business into reform. He exposed, for instance, that J. P. Morgan had failed the pay taxes for years, and forced New York Stock Exchange president Richard Whitney to admit to the existence of "pools" that manipulated stock prices. Pecora later recounted the difficulty of achieving the reforms that are the basis for modern securities laws:

> **Virtually no aid or cooperation came from the denizens of that great marketplace we euphemistically call Wall Street. Indeed they were passed in the face of the bitter and powerfully organized opposition of the financial community. That opposition was overcome principally because public indignation had been deeply aroused by the conclusive evidence of wrongdoing.**[4]

Certainly, the fact that U.S. financial history has seen more than its fair share of white collar scandal is scant solace to those who lost money in the post-Enron world. But as we will see, investors should be encouraged by the alacrity with which America's policymakers, securities exchanges, and companies sought reform to restore the public's confidence in our economic system.

Sarbanes-Oxley and Good Corporate Governance

Wall Street was, of course, particularly hard hit by 9/11. The aftermath of the tragic events of that day were made all the more depressing in the months that followed by the growing revelations about Wall Street's complicity in the sorry state of the economy and the markets.

It started with energy producer and trader Enron. At one time the seventh largest company in the United States, Enron provided journalists examples of all that ailed corporate America: fraudulent financial statements, biased Wall Street research, sold-out accounting services, and feckless board oversight. Unfortunately, subsequent developments at companies like WorldCom and Adelphia made it impossible to argue that the system was not in need of massive reform and government oversight. Responding to the risk of a complete loss of confidence in America's capital markets, the Bush administration and Congress sought to gain control of the situation. The SEC, headed at the time by Harvey Pitt, took the unusual step of forcing the CEOs and CFOs of the nation's largest 947 companies to personally vouch for their financial statements. Congress quickly followed the commission's lead and passed the historic Sarbanes-Oxley bill.

In perhaps the greatest expansion of government influence into the affairs of business since the New Deal, the new law leveled a broadside against the accounting industry. It established the Public Company Accounting Oversight Board, forced board audit committees to be totally independent of management, banned accounting firms from offering management consulting services to their audit clients, quickened disclosure of insider sales, forced CEOs and CFOs to certify their financial statements, and nearly doubled the budget of the SEC.

The new law was not without its critics. Some suggested, for instance, that the new reforms fundamentally weakened the structure of the limited liability of the corporation, which was the basis for money and credit for centuries. But an interesting if little noticed development occurred after the SEC action was put forth: Companies began to do the right thing on their own. Remarkably, despite the cost and the potential risk, a number of companies that had not been required in the action to certify their financial results began to do so anyway. Others, like Coca-Cola, began to unilaterally expense options without being forced to do so. This was encouraging, for it suggested that at least some companies within the free market system were willing to compete with one another for investors' funds on a new front— a reputation for corporate responsibility.

Perhaps even more encouraging, the market also bottomed in October 2002, less than three months after Sarbanes-Oxley was passed. There was certainly no shortage of doomsday scenarios or naysayers at the time, but little by little the new laws and the new focus on corporate responsibility helped individual and institutional investors realize that while massive reforms were necessary on Wall Street, corporate America, and the accounting industry, the vast majority of companies in the country were run by responsible and honorable men and women.

Yet despite the subsequent recovery in the economy and the markets, many still wonder today how it was possible for Enron to defraud both the professional and individual investor alike in a system built on the rule of law. There are no easy answers to this question. Some believe it is a problem inherent in capitalism itself. Others see the corporate malfeasance of the late 1990s as a natural outgrowth of the investment environment of the 1980s, when a hostile takeover culture encouraged boards of directors to coddle managements by adopting a slew of protections for them—including poison pill defenses, golden parachutes, and staggered boards.[5] As eminent financial journalist Roger Lowenstein put it in a piece on Adelphia in the *New York Times Magazine,* "However badly the Rigases [the company's founders] behaved, they were helped along the way by lenders and investment bankers, auditors, lawyers, analysts—just about anyone whose job it should have been to protect the public."[6]

There may be a disheartening element of truth in all of the above explanations, but it should be noted that past scandals have inevitably led to reforms that have made our financial markets and, by extension, our economy stronger. Further, the turmoil and resulting reform following such periods has often presented both individual and institutional investors with new and exciting investment opportunities.

In this regard, market historians are likely to view the activist role pursued by the administration and Congress as important turning points in the war against corporate skulduggery. At the very least, the ensuing reforms laid the foundation for the quick turnaround in the markets and the economy in 2003. While there is undoubtedly much progress still to be made, companies and brokerage firms are now encouraging shareholders to look at stocks as they once did—as long-term investments. Perhaps more encouraging, as we will see in the next section, a number of companies have been established in recent years to help investors do just that.

An Investor's Checklist: Warning Signals

Of course, the importance of character in the world of high finance came stunningly back to the fore after 9/11, the ensuing recession, and the revelations about seemingly widespread corporate corruption after the bubble burst. If Wall Street has taught me only one thing, it's that you can't legislate morality. Remarkably, the emphasis on corporate governance, while perhaps appearing woefully inadequate today, compares quite favorably to the sorry state of shareholder rights in past generations.

While it might be hard to believe, given the preponderance of corporate shenanigans and scandals over the last few years, America's public companies and its securities markets are among the most heavily regulated in the world. Until recently, instances of true shareholder activism were remarkably rare and were addressed only after a firm's value had been compromised. In one such case, Sir Bernard Docker was ousted from his perch at BSA/Daimler in 1955 when rumors about his extravagant lifestyle on the company's dime came to light in the City of London.[7] Ultimately, however, shareholders dissatisfied with the responsiveness of managers to their needs were left with little choice but to vote with their feet, as it were, and sell their shares.

To again quote John Kenneth Galbraith in *A Short History of Financial Euphoria*:

> **Regulation outlawing financial incredulity or mass euphoria is not a practical possibility. If applied generally to such human condition, the result would be an impressive, perhaps oppressive, and certainly ineffective body of law. The only remedy, in fact, is an enhanced skepticism that would resolutely associate too evident optimism with probable foolishness and that would not associate intelligence with the acquisition, the deployment, or, for that matter, the administration of large sums of money.[8]**

In essence, determining the truthfulness of management or its interest in its own investors is up to the shareholder himself. The trick is for investors not to rely on their "stars" but on themselves, by establishing simple yet rigorous tests that prove the companies they are interested in buying are serious about corporate governance.

This is not a simple matter. Metrics to determine the accountability of companies to their shareholders are often as varied and complex as the companies themselves. New York–based GovernanceMetrics International, for one, attempts to answer 600 questions about a company's board, its structure, and its responsiveness to shareholders in order to come up with its GMI ratings of corporate behavior. And while GovernanceMetrics and a few other new companies provide corporate governance rankings to high-paying institutional money managers, individual investors are largely on their own. However, though few individual shareholders have the time to engage in the in-depth research required to get a true window into the soul of a corporation, or have the money to purchase the services of companies designed for this purpose, there are a number of warning signs that should give investors pause. We will discuss them below.

The Sold-Out or Feckless Board of Directors

It goes without saying that managements might find it difficult to satisfy the disparate needs of all of the constituencies attempting to influence today's large publicly traded company. The interests of shareholders, the work force, and federal, state, and local governments must be considered. But insisting on a consensus among all of these groups before acting would hamstring managers from quickly taking advantage of opportunities in an increasingly fast-paced and global marketplace.

Managers are hired in the first place to draw upon their experience and expertise to take risks and make decisions that might have little initial support among shareholders. But how do shareholders give managers the latitude to act quickly and yet ensure that they are acting in the best interests of the shareholder? Carrying on a tradition established in the earliest forms of corporate organization in Great Britain and the American colonies, the board of directors bridges the gap between the owners of the corporation (the shareholders) and those entrusted with maximizing its value (management). To quote corporate governance legends Robert Monks and Neil Minow in their seminal work on the subject:

> **In theory at least, the law imposes on the board a strict and absolute fiduciary duty to ensure that a company is run in the**

long-term interests of the owners, the shareholders ... boards are the overlap between the small, powerful group that runs the company and the huge, diffuse, and relatively powerless group that simply wished to see the company run well.[9]

Ultimately, investors should monitor the composition and effectiveness of the board, which is entrusted with ensuring that managements are accountable to the shareholders. Unfortunately, there are no hard and fast rules to determine whether the board is serving the best interests of the shareholders or of the managements that work for them. Making matters more difficult, management often proposes new board members to serve, and even counts the votes that elect them. Again, the goal for shareholders is to have a board that can look at the various issues affecting the corporation with equanimity and without the psychological and emotional baggage of longstanding relationships with management. To this end, there are several questions investors should ask themselves about the boards of the companies in which they invest:

- Are any of the board's members related to management?
- Do they sit on other boards or run other companies that might present obvious conflicts of interest with their role as stewards of the corporation?
- Are they former officers of the company?
- How entrenched are members of the board? Are there term limits for board members?
- How often does the board meet?
- Does the board meet in the absence of executive directors?

A sample of the questions GovernanceMetrics uses to determine the independence of the board can be seen in Table 4-1.

While there have been countless examples in recent years of incompetent and ineffective boards, perhaps one of the worst examples of the phenomenon of the sold-out board was at RJR Nabisco in the 1980s, later recounted in one of the best period pieces of the era, *Barbarians at the Gate*. CEO Tylee Wilson spent nearly $70 million developing a smokeless cigarette without bothering to inform the board. The project ultimately proved to be disastrous for the company and for Wilson. Unfortunately, things didn't get any better with the appointment of a new chief executive, F. Ross Johnson, who used company funds to buy the acquiescence of the board with the use of corporate jets, outsized compensation, and country club memberships.[10]

TABLE 4-1 GovernanceMetrics International's Sample Questions to Determine Board Independence

1. Does the company disclose the criteria used by the board or a board committee to formaly evaluate CEO performance?
2. Does a committee of the board evaluate the performance of the board on a regular basis?
3. Does each board committee undertake an evaluation of its own performance on a regualr basis?
4. Is it the board's policy to hold meetings of the nonexecutive directors before or after every board meeting?
5. Is training and orientation required for new board members?
6. Does the board have a policy concerning directors whose principal occupation has changed?
7. Is there a limit to the total number of years an individual is able to serve as a board member, or is there a limit to the number of times a director is allowed to be re-elected to the board?
8. Have any directors served on the board for fifteen years or more?
9. Has there been a related-party transaction involving the chairman, CEO, president, COO, or CFO or a relative within the last three years?
10. Has the number of company shares held by the senior management decreased by 10 percent or more over the last twelve months?

While the problems at Tyco, Enron, and other companies have emboldened advocates of good corporate governance to call for board reform, many have suggested that it is unrealistic to expect directors to act as true fiduciaries when they are paid, on average, $50,000 a year for attending a handful of meetings. Robert Monks believes that "the key to a good board is ownership. Each director's personal worth should be closely tied to the fortunes of the company. No director is going to remain passive if a quarter or even a tenth of his net worth is at stake."[11] Ultimately, companies should seek independent board members whose long-term interests are matched with those of the shareholders.

Excessive Executive Compensation

Perhaps one of the best ways to determine the effectiveness and vigilance of the board is to see how it compensates the corporation's top executives. Smart individual and professional investors alike realize that talented managers cost money. However, the tendency of some companies to overcompensate executives for less than stellar performances is disturbing to many. It's hard to believe that the average of any group of individuals could make $12 million a year, but by the year 2000 the average CEO of a big corporation in America took home just that—about four times as much as in 1990.[12] Standout executives received pay packages that were totally divorced from the reality of their worth in the marketplace.

While overpaying managerial talent is one thing, it was the nature of the compensation—stock options—that ultimately provided executives with incentives to pursue strategies to boost the stock price in the short term rather than to increase the value of the corporation for shareholders over the long term. Ostensibly designed to encourage managers to act like owners, many boards chose the then relatively new compensation tool of options to attract managerial talent in the 1980s takeover binge. By the year 2000, equity-based compensation rose to about 60 percent of CEO pay versus about 5 percent in 1990, and concurrently, a company's stock price became the all-important metric of executive performance. The SEC made matters worse when it allowed insiders to sell stock as early as the same day they exercised the underlying options. Previously, managers were required to hold shares for at least six months under Rule 16b of the Securities and Exchange Act.[13]

Because corporations weren't required to expense stock options expenses on their income statement, companies fed the speculative fever of the day by liberally granting options at every turn. With the benefit of hindsight, option-based compensation, which appeared to be a win-win for both shareholders and management, turned out be so lucrative that it provided an incentive for management not to act as owners, but as renters. And ultimately the fallen stars of the business world turned out to be the worst kind of renter—like a group of guys who stop at Hertz before a bachelor party weekend in Vegas. Warren Buffett has suggested that companies do away with the practice altogether, preferring instead to compensate managements with stock (owners) rather than options (renters).

Investors should ask tough questions about how a company's top executives are compensated before they invest:

- Is the compensation stock or option based?
- Over what time period do these grants vest?
- Does the company expense stock options?
- Do only nonexecutive members of the board set compensation levels for top executives?
- How does the CEO's pay compare with others in the same industry?

Ultimately, investors should seek companies that are willing to pay for top managerial talent but that structure compensation schemes to reward the long-term commitment and performance of its executives.

Poison Pills, Golden Parachutes, and Antitakeover Provisions

Another outgrowth of the takeover boom in the 1980s was the development of corporate structures and policies designed to protect management and to thwart potential acquirers. The growth of the junk bond market allowed corporate raiders like T. Boone Pickens, Carl Icahn, and Sir James Goldsmith to use debt to finance the purchase of their potential takeover targets. Striking fear in the hearts of top executives in corporate America throughout the decade, the raiders would fire management and shed assets to pay for the debt immediately upon completion of the deal.

In an effort to stanch hostile deals and to hold onto their jobs, top executives, with the participation of the board, often sought to raise the potential costs of an acquisition. New terms used to describe these takeover defenses were introduced into the already rich lexicon of Wall Street. A typical example of a "poison pill," for instance, might be for a takeover target to issue a new series of preferred stock that gives shareholders the right to redeem it at a premium price after a takeover, greatly increasing the cost of a deal to potential acquirers. "Golden parachutes" often give top executives lavish perquisites and outsized bonuses if they lost their jobs as the result of a merger or acquisition.

Companies also decided to stagger the election of the boards. Until the mid-1980s the slate of directors was often voted on, en masse, at the annual meeting. But with the increasing likelihood of takeovers in the latter half of the decade, many companies started to nominate directors for three staggered sets of three-year terms. This way, potential suitors would need to run a dissident slate of directors for three years running to gain full control of the board. The practice became exceedingly common in the takeover era, with nearly 50 percent of U.S. companies adopting the practice by 1991, up from roughly a third in 1986.[14] Perhaps hard to believe for the uninitiated, Delaware, with its strong antitakeover legislation, also became the destination of choice for incorporation.

It's not easy to be on the side of guys like Carl Icahn. And though the takeover boom and the rise to prominence of the corporate raider in the late 1980s was particularly vexing for employees and certain specific communities, it did put management on notice that they could actually be held accountable for their performance. Such "market for control" issues, as they are deemed in the corporate governance world, are among the most sensitive and tricky for investors to understand and decipher. On the one hand, good managers should be protected from the potentially disrupting and less than altruistic intentions of corporate raiders. On the other, strong antitakeover structures might allow managements to become untouchable and prevent shareholders from fully realizing the true value of their shares.

Unfortunately, the trend of such practices has clearly been advantagous to management. Despite decades of slow and steady progress in bolstering the rights of shareholders, the stock market boom weakened any sense of urgency for reform. In fact, by 2000, one out of 10 American companies were incorporated in Delaware, a state notorious for favoring management over shareholders.[15] Some companies, like Boeing and Maytag, actually decided to keep antitakeover poison pills even after shareholders voted them down in recent years,[16] and almost every company has antitakeover provisions on its books these days. But investors should take notice of how responsive companies are to shareholders who wish to effect change.

The existence of a fair price provision, which requires potential acquirers to pay the same price for all shares bought, not just for those shares needed to gain control, is one indication that managers are adopting a poison pill provision for the right rather than the wrong reason. The "White Knight" strategy, which seeks another friendly acquirer in the face of a hostile bid, is another shareholder-friendly defense. Ultimately, investors need to determine whether such defenses are designed to thwart not only takeovers, but also shareholder influence on management and on the board.

Earnings Restatements and the Recurring Nonrecurring Charge

The quarterly earnings statement is the main point of contact for most retail and even some institutional investors with the company. In the days before the SEC, financial disclosure was largely up to the company itself. This is a major reason why dividends were so much more important to investors in those days—the dividend check was one of the few tangible pieces of evidence that the company was actually making money.

With the birth of the SEC and more stringent listing requirements of the New York Stock Exchange, the National Association of Securities Dealers, and other regulatory bodies, companies were required to provide certified financial statements and at least some minimal level of financial disclosure. But although companies are required to follow Generally Accepted Accounting Principles (GAAP) when drafting their financial statements, the increasingly competitive nature of business in general, and the accounting industry specifically, has prompted a number of companies (as we saw in the late 1990s with Enron, Worldcom, and others) to play fast and loose with accounting rules.

If truth be told, wading through the maze of modern financial statements requires a level of training and time that few individual investors have. Even professional investors come across financial statements from time to time that are nearly impossible to decipher. Warren Buffett once quipped that he would give all business school students a final exam in which they would have to value an Internet company. The companies were so difficult to value, he said, that any student actually providing an answer would automatically fail.

For all of the complexity of financial statements today, however, there is one way in which investors of all levels can quickly determine whether a company possesses good financial controls and is doing its best to fully disclose its financial condition: the degree to which a company restates earnings. No practice is potentially more harmful or deceiving to investors as the nonrecurring recurring charge to earnings. While restructuring charges are difficult for the average investor to understand, it becomes easier when one remembers that economic earnings are not the same as accounting earnings. Again relying on the oracle of good corporate governance, Robert Monks:

> **Imagine a company that has reported over the past five years earnings of $10 a share each year; then in year six, the company decides on a restructuring charge of $75 a share. During all of the six-year period, the company is deemed to be operating profitably from an accounting point of view. Each year it has its $10 earnings; the retroactive "restructuring charge" cannot affect the five years of perceptions that have passed. Furthermore, because it is a restructuring charge, it does not alter the reported "earnings from ongoing operations" in year six, which are, let's say, $10 a share. Thus, the company has lost money over a six-year period, and yet each annual component shows a profit at the time of reporting.[17]**

As the bull market continued to roar through the 1990s, and investors became less rigorous in their examination of earnings, companies would often simply exclude these write-offs from their calculations, claiming that investors would be misled by these immaterial "nonrecurring" charges. These new "pro forma" earnings, it was claimed, were the only numbers investors should use when valuing the company. Sadly, companies began to expand the definition of "onetime" charges to include expenses that were clearly part of the day-to-day operations of the company. The practice became so widespread that some even suggested that "pro forma" earnings should actually be called EBBS or "earnings before bad stuff." Warren Buffett noted that while earnings for the Fortune 500 companies were $324 billion in 1997, total charges from items such as asset writedowns and restructurings were actually $86 billion in 1998, or a stunning 26 percent.

Overlay recurring "nonrecurring" charges with the obscurity of expensing stock options and pension accounting, and it's little wonder that the little guy has increasingly thrown up his hands in disgust. In an effort to help investors through the maze that had become modern financial statements, the SEC passed Regulation G as a follow-on to the Sarbanes-Oxley legislation. While the new rule in no way prevents companies from applying pro-forma conventions in the calculation of earnings, it does require companies to clearly reconcile the differences between Generally Accepted Accounting Principles and other accounting conventions, specifically pro forma. In addition, the measure will prohibit material misstatements or omissions that would make the presentation of non-GAAP data misleading. While both companies and analysts have begun to apply more conservative accounting practices in their calculation of earnings and estimates, Regulation G offers an additional step that will allow investors to more accurately compare companies across industries and sectors.

While a renewed focus on corporate governance and new legislation has narrowed the differences between "operating" and reported earnings in recent years, companies have a long way to go (see Chart 4-1).

Ultimately, investors should remember that frequent earnings restatements may mean that a company has weak internal financial controls or that it is purposely manipulating the investing public's opinion about its financial condition. In either case, it is a bad sign.

The Inconvenient Shareholders Meeting

One of the best ways to get some idea of management's attitude toward its shareholders is to attend a company's annual meeting. While this may seem hopelessly passé in an age of instantaneous com-

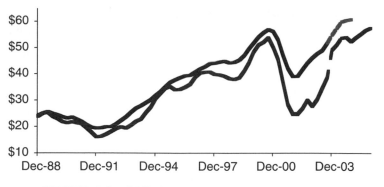

CHART 4-1 S&P 500 Operating EPS vs. Reported EPS in Dollars

munication, it's never a bad idea to see management in action. With the possible exception of CNBC, the shareholder's meeting may be as close as an individual investor can get to management. Because large institutional investors have as much access to management as they need, many of them consider these meetings a complete waste of time. But it's hard to believe that professional investors wouldn't be well served to see management's attitudes toward the little guy once in a while.

One of the first tests the average investor can apply to the annual meeting is its location. If XYZ decides to hold its meeting in Moose Jaw, Saskatchewan, in mid-February, chances are pretty good that management doesn't want to be asked too many questions from the people who actually own the company.

Another warning sign for those who want managers to work for their best interests: In what should be considered the ultimate act of management arrogance, many top officers skip the shareholders' meeting altogether and send underlings instead. Who do these officers work for if not for the shareholder?

If, on the other hand, management appears to actually want individual investors to attend the annual meeting, widely advertising its time and place, one might assume that management has little to hide. In this regard, perhaps its not surprising that the richest and arguably best CEO in the country, Warren Buffett, puts on a show for his shareholders every year, arranging picnics, softball games, and dinners for them in between presentations. The annual gathering has become so popular in recent years that the company has had to rent out Aksarben Stadium in downtown Omaha (seating 11,000) to accommodate all of its guests.

Why No Dividend?

As we discussed in Chapter 1, several generations of discriminatory tax treatment and corporate greed have taught investors to think of their returns from common stocks solely in price terms, as opposed to the combination of the returns from both prices and dividends. Of course, not all companies can or should pay dividends in their infancy as public companies, needing all available capital to build a business. But at the very least, all investors should require a thorough explanation of how a company's earnings are being employed. After a while, companies should either distribute the income earned or have a very good reason for retaining it. For too long, shareholders cared little about how a company was using its earnings as long as the stock was going up. Managements incorrectly assumed that shareholder apathy gave them carte blanche to do whatever they wanted.

Many companies also suggested that the mere act of paying a dividend would brand them as slow growers, raising their cost of capital and limiting their ability to raise new capital. This culture of greed came to an abrupt end when the revelations about Enron and others came to light. All of a sudden many shareholders realized that the companies in which they were investing weren't being managed for their benefit, but rather, for the enrichment of management. Two of the best performing companies in the S&P 500 in 2003, Best Buy and Mandalay Bay, actually initiated a dividend last year. That is not to say that dividends are the be all and end all of good corporate citizenship, but they're a start.

The Cockroach Theory

Good investment analysts have long believed in the "cockroach theory" when it came to earnings disappointments. That is to say, big earnings misses usually lead to subsequent shortfalls and are often a good reason to sell the stock. It's safe to say that this theory can be applied to shortfalls in good corporate governance as well. In today's volatile financial markets, failing to act quickly at the first whiff of financial impropriety can be extremely costly.

The performance of Tyco after the bubble burst is a great case in point. At the start of 2002, the SEC first began looking into questions about the accuracy of Tyco's bookkeeping and accounting. Of course, it was easy to shrug off the charges and attribute them to an overzealous SEC. But in six months, from January to July 2002, the stock would fall from $34 to $8. The moral: When in doubt, get out.

Good Corporate Governance Outperforms

A 2003 study by McKinsey & Company found that 76 percent of institutional investors would pay a premium for companies that were serious about corporate governance issues. While this makes a lot of sense, serious students of financial history know that conventional wisdom can often be a poor predictor of market performance. And although it makes perfect sense that investors should seek out those companies that treat their shareholders with respect, it would be foolish to assume that they would outperform without further careful research. Fortunately, a series of new academic studies have provided evidence that good corporate governance can indeed lead to superior portfolio performance.

In their paper "Corporate Governance and Equity Prices," Paul Gompers and Joy Ishii at Harvard, and Andrew Metrick at Wharton, sought to determine the value-added of good corporate governance in equity portfolios. Using data from the Investor Responsibility Research Center to study 24 key signs of good corporate citizenship, Gompers et al. created a "Governance Index" to rank 1,500 large firms during the 1990s. Their findings are stunning, suggesting not only that good corporate governance actually was worth something to shareholders, but also that its value was actually growing.

In 1990, each one-point improvement in their Governance Index added 2.2 percent to a firm's value. By the end of the decade, each one-point improvement in the index was worth 11.4 percent. Perhaps not surprisingly, a strategy that bought those firms with the strongest shareholder rights (deemed "democracies" by the researchers) and sold those firms with the weakest rights (deemed "dictatorships") provided excess returns of 8.5 percent a year between 1990 and 1998. What's more, those companies with the best records of looking out for shareholder interests had higher market capitalizations, profits, and sales growth rates than those with the worst records. They also had lower capital expenditures and made few corporate acquisitions.[18]

One of the great testaments to the strength of our capitalist system is that a number of companies have sprung up in response to the more dramatic corporate scandals of the last few years to provide some clarity in the often murky waters of corporate governance. The aforementioned GovernanceMetrics, based in New York City, for example, provides governance scores on more than 2,000 companies in the United States and on companies abroad. By answering nearly 600 questions concerning all manner of shareholder friendly issues, the company takes on the labor intensive process of determining whether a company that "talks the talk" on corporate governance actually "walks the walk." Of course, there are plenty of companies that do neither. GovernanceMetrics has also found that companies with good corporate governance outperform those with bad records of corporate citizenship (see Chart 4-2). Perhaps more specifically, they found that while there is no guarantee that companies with good corporate governance will provide outsized returns, companies with bad governance often disappoint investors.

The Need to Take the Long View

It might be hard to believe, but stocks represent the longest duration financial assets an investor can purchase. Theoretically, they can remain in an investor's portfolio forever. And yet, ironically, shareholders have been encouraged by brokers and sometimes the companies themselves to look at stocks as a short-term path to riches rather than a long-term road to wealth.

This is true for both the average and professional investors. The complexity of corporate structures and financial statements makes the individual investor exceedingly susceptible to company and Wall Street hype. And the growing competitiveness of the money management business, together with the increasingly short-term nature upon which portfolio managers are judged, forces many professional investors to choose between staying employed and their long-term roles as fiduciaries.

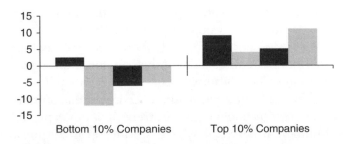

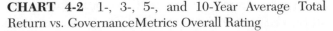

CHART 4-2 1-, 3-, 5-, and 10-Year Average Total Return vs. GovernanceMetrics Overall Rating

The sad fact of the matter is that a guy like Warren Buffett, possessing the intestinal fortitude to withstand inevitable periods of underperformance for the greater good of his shareholders, would have been fired countless times if he had decided to work within the confines of the mutual fund industry. "You've had some great years, Warren. But the numbers speak for themselves. We're losing assets. I'm sorry." And let's face it, in some shops Buffett would have been lucky to escape physical harm in late 1999 or early 2000 when he sat on the tech boom sidelines. Of course, there's nothing wrong with attempting to consistently beat the market in an effort to build wealth. But aside from Bill Miller of Legg Mason and a handful of others, who among us can time the market successfully over time?

The trick for both groups is to pay attention to how companies actually treat them. In this regard, good corporate governance is a far better indication of the potential to build long-term wealth than a quarterly earnings release.

Key Take-Aways

1. When making the decision to buy and sell a company's stock, determining a company's responsiveness to its shareholders is becoming as important as a company's financial statements.
2. Directors should lack obvious conflicts of interest with the companies on whose boards they sit. But with the exception of requiring directors to hold a significant portion of their net worth in the company's stock, there are few fail-safe ways to ensure a board's independence from management.
3. Excessive and undisclosed executive compensation might signal that management is more interested in its own wealth than creating wealth for its shareholders. Stock options make managers "renters" rather than "owners" of a company's stock and can encourage short-term risk-taking over a long-term approach of creating shareholder value.
4. Strong antitakeover provisions such as staggered boards and poison pill defenses limit a shareholder's ability to hold management accountable for its actions.
5. Frequent earnings restatements may mean that a company has weak internal financial controls or is purposely manipulating the investing public's opinion about its financial condition. In either case, it is a bad sign. Remember that bad numbers take longer to add up than good numbers, and the Cockroach Theory: big

earnings misses usually lead subsequent shortfalls and are often a good reason to sell the stock.

6. The annual shareholders' meeting gives both the professional and individual investor some insights into management's interest in its investors. Out-of-the-way annual shareholders meetings at inconvenient times may suggest that a company has something to hide.

7. New academic studies have proven what many individual and professional investors have known all along: Good corporate governance practices boost stock returns.

5

WINNER–TAKE–ALL MARKETS

THE IMPACT OF FREE TRADE AND TECHNOLOGY ON INVESTORS, COMPANIES, AND WORKERS

"Fortune favors the brave."

—VIRGIL, *THE AENEID*

As THE POLITICAL ADVERTISEMENTS in this year's presidential campaign have so often pointed out, American companies, workers, and investors have to deal with the threats and opportunities from technological innovation and free trade with greater and greater frequency. Certainly, today's fights for market share are extraordinarily intense. After a Perfect Storm of sorts for the U.S. economy, consisting of 9/11, the corporate malfeasance scandals, and a recession, corporate managers have had to become increasingly creative and tough to protect their place in the world economy.

In this regard, it is no coincidence that Wal-Mart has become the country's largest company in terms of sales, or that Dell's low-cost business model for PCs has largely driven its chief competitors into other businesses, or that China's economy has grown from relative obscurity 25 years ago to a global player today. Michael Dell may have summed up the new character of global commerce best when commenting on Dell Computer's reluctance to pursue acquisitions: "You get a lot of bad stuff when you acquire other companies and I'm not sure we need it. The best approach for us is to acquire our competitors' customers *one at a time*."

In fact, presidents have little control over the difficulty of companies to maintain competitive advantages, or their inability to raise prices or maintain profit margins, or the increasing insecurity of American workers. These are largely the result of secular forces: the changing social contract between companies and workers, globalization, and technological innovation. Neither political party says much about these realities, yet candidates who don't mention them are incapable of defending their virtues. As we will see in this chapter, the increasingly competitive nature of global commerce, contrary to public opinion, actually works to the benefit of American workers and consumers due to the strength of the U.S. political and economic system.

Globalization and the Modern Corporation

The utopian vision of the corporation—one in which it could serve the needs of both its shareholders and the community with equal aplomb, only existed, if it ever existed at all, for a relatively short period of time after World War II, when America stood alone on the world stage, its industrial base intact and its military dominance assured,

Little by little, America's dominance of the global economy started to wane, as a combination of liberalized trade policies and technological innovation made foreign economies stronger and the world seemingly a lot smaller. The global corporation got a further boost with the fall of the Berlin Wall in 1990, opening up well-educated societies to the concepts of democracy and capitalism. This was partly by design. Implicit in America's massive foreign aid programs in the postwar years was the hope that economic prosperity would not only foster democracy, but also provide foreign markets for U.S. companies.

Free trade and technological innovation led to the massive expansion of U.S. companies operating internationally. Between 1975 and 2001 their number quintupled, to 65,000, with revenues of $19 trillion. These companies employed 54 million people worldwide and operated 850,000 foreign affiliates.[1]

The dramatic impact the rise of multinational companies and the expansion of free trade can have on local economies has not gone unnoticed by antiglobalization groups. Although it's not uncommon to see antiglobalization groups, who through fear, ignorance, or self-interest protest against the growing power of multinational companies, in fact almost all nonlocal industries are subject to both the opportunities and the risks presented by global commerce. The concept of the corporation in general, and of the public company in particular, rests on the expectation that its managers will seek to maximize its share-holders' return on investment. In this sense it is, ultimately, democratic. I believe that a dispassionate view of the facts would lead to the conclusion that there have been few developments as beneficial to the ordinary man on the street or the distribution of global economic growth than the creation of the modern international corporation.

The idea that large multinational companies are somehow involved in some nefarious subterranean plot to wrest control from popularly elected governments and keep the peoples of the nonindustrialized world in poverty is, to my mind, so patently ridiculous as to barely warrant mentioning. Certainly, it would be difficult to suggest to many executives in America's auto industry or to its erstwhile television manufacturers. Most U.S. companies would be happy to maintain whatever market share they have now—much less seek to expand it.

Perhaps as a consequence of free trade and the bare-knuckled foreign competition it brings, global markets have only intensified the changing fortunes of America's companies. The pace at which companies left the Fortune 500, for example, increased nearly four times between 1970 and 1990.[2] It was in this environment that a new breed of manager—intensely competitive and seemingly unencumbered with Victorian notions of responsibility toward labor and society—was born. To a large extent the celebrity CEOs of the 1980s and 1990s—Al Dunlap of Sunbeam, Jack Welch of General Electric, and Lou Gerstner of IBM—made their bones not as innovators, but as cost cutters.

The hypercompetitive nature of global markets can, of course, be enormously unsettling for employees and local communities. But it would be a mistake to assume this is a weakness in America's system. It can result in difficult times for those affected, but America's flexibility allows it to bounce back quickly from even the most wrenching economic times. Perhaps the greatest testament to the benefits of this sometimes harsh flexibility was the quick snap-back in profits in 2003 after corporate America's Perfect Storm of 9/11, the corporate malfeasance scandals, and the recession over the last three years.

In their brief but thorough history of the joint-stock company, authors John Mickelthwait and Adrian Wooldridge sum it up by saying that "multinationals will continue to represent much of what is best about companies: their capacity to improve productivity and therefore the living standards of ordinary people. But they will also continue to embody what is most worrying—perhaps most alienating—about companies as well."[3]

The New 800-Pound Gorilla: China

In many ways, China has come to exemplify the opportunities and risks inherent in today's increasingly interconnected global economy. In much the same way Sam Walton built Wal-Mart into the largest retailer in the world by offering value through scale and distribution efficiency, China is systematically using its low cost labor and rapidly expanding production and technology skills to manufacture inexpensive but competitive products.

China is rapidly entering new markets, increasing productivity, limiting pricing power, and taking market share not only in the United States, but also around the world. The last time one nation had such a large impact on both global growth and inflation came in the nineteenth century, when the United States grew from an emerging market into a global powerhouse. But unlike the world economy of more than a century ago, technological advances and modern transportation have made commerce truly global, and allowed China to establish itself as a player on the world economic stage in a relatively short period of time.

Since Deng Xiaoping began to rebuild China's economy on market-based principles in 1978, the country's growth has been nothing short of breathtaking. At that time, China's economy was the ninth largest in the world, with a total gross domestic product just one-eighth that of the United States and one-third that of Japan. By 2001, China had become the world's second largest economy, with 40 percent of its workers in private or foreign enterprises—up from zero 25 years ago—and a GDP about half that of the United States and 60 percent larger than Japan's. According to the Federal Reserve Bank of Dallas, based on current growth rates China will overtake the United States as the world's largest economy within 12 years.[4]

One of the odd features of China's industrial revolution is that while it will likely result in significant inflationary pressures in raw materials like oil, coal, and steel, it's also likely to lead to global disinflation. How can this be so?

First, in an effort to avoid undue social pressures resulting from the migration of agricultural workers to its cities, China is being forced to rapidly expand its infrastructure to support its growing industrial base. And, unlike America in the nineteenth century, China is a huge net importer of raw materials. With a growth rate of 9.1 percent in 2003, China consumed a remarkable 50 percent of the world's cement, 30 percent of its coal, and more than a third of its steel. Its copper imports rose 15 percent, and its nickel imports doubled.[5] There is little doubt that the strength in energy and raw materials prices in the last few years will be directly attributable to China's rapid economic growth.

Second, China's role as the global engine for disinflation rests with its oversupply of cheap labor. With 1.3 billion people, its population is 4.5 times that of the United States, and its work force is six times as great. The result of these disparities is all the more striking when one considers that China's manufacturing wages are just 4 percent of U.S. wages and only 29 percent of those in Mexico: 61 cents an hour in China, versus $16.14 in the United States and $2.08 in Mexico.[6]

The transformation of China from an agrarian society into a truly modern economic powerhouse will present American companies, workers, and investors with some of their most significant challenges and opportunities in the next century.

For American companies, it seems clear that the China miracle is no flash in the pan. As Chart 5-1 indicates, China is already the chief exporter to the United States of everything from PCs to toys to audio equipment to men's footwear.[7] One can only assume that its membership in the World Trade Organization in 2002 will accelerate its ability to take market share from other industrialized and emerging economies in a wide array of industries. As a result, China's growing manufacturing might is likely to affect American

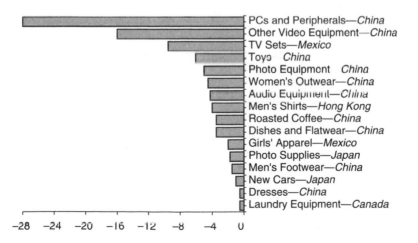

CHART 5-1 Top Exporters (Countries) to U.S. among Goods with Greatest Five-Year Price Decline

companies, which strive for ever-lower levels of costs and ever-higher levels of productivity.

This may seem like bad news for American workers. Given the fact that labor costs comprise two-thirds of the total cost of goods sold by the average American company, China's vast supply of labor will undoubtedly be seen by U.S. corporations as an opportunity too good to pass up when it comes to low value-added manufacturing processes. But it would be a mistake to view China's economic growth as a threat to American jobs. While the media has highlighted the impact of outsourcing on American workers (more on this in the next section), little has been said about China's potential as an end-market for U.S. goods and services.

As China exports more, its standard of living will undoubtedly rise, and its ability to buy foreign goods and services will increase. There are signs that this is already happening. China's imports as a percent of GDP have grown from just 2 percent in 1970 to almost 25 percent in 2002.[8] The opportunities presented by a growing consumer class in China are even more compelling when one considers the current low standard of living of Chinese consumers (Table 5-1).

Finally, what I noted above that might seem like bad news for American workers will be seen in a different way by investors. To them, the implications of China's ascendance on U.S. companies is more clear: those that can successfully take advantage of the China

TABLE 5-1   Goods per 1,000 People

PRODUCT	CHINA	U.S.
Bicycles	583	361
Motorcycles	22	15
Autos	6	475
Telephone Main Lines	137	667
Mobile Phones	110	451
Radios	339	2,117
Televisions	304	835
Cable TV Subscribers	69	257
Living Space (sq. feet per capita)	66	718
Electric Power Consumption (kw-hours per capita)	827	12,322

Source: Federal Reserve Bank of Dallas

miracle will have enormous opportunities to drive down costs, increase productivity, and increase profits, while those that cannot will be staring at an increasingly competitive and harsh economic environment in the years to come.

Of course, there are cynics. Some of the statistics on China seem so otherworldly that many people doubt the China miracle. After all, they ask, isn't growth in China whatever its leaders say it is? Indeed, in terms of freedom, human rights, and financial transparency, China unquestionably has a long way to go. But if the numbers are even half correct, the country's effort to join the world's industrialized nations will be a phenomenon too big to ignore.

Free Trade and the Outsourcing Myth

Former Prime Minister of Britain Benjamin Disraeli once said, "There are lies, damn lies, and statistics." To a surprising degree in modern politics, the increasingly partisan nature of our political system leads politicians of both political parties to distort facts about the economy. Buried in a wide array of statistics, the media, sadly, often accepts these distortions as fact, making it difficult for regular people who don't deal in such minutiae to determine just where the truth ends and politics begins. Perhaps more rife for demagoguery than any other issue in this year's presidential campaign, outsourcing has become the latest cause célèbre for aspiring politicians and media pundits alike.

The images on the nightly news are familiar—a padlocked chain-link fence around a plant in a "Rust Belt" state, a long line at the unemployment insurance office, and a glistening modern manufacturing facility in some emerging market. While there may be an element of truth in these images, what is unfortunately not being said is that this process of "creative destruction" is nothing new and is the basis for our economic system.

The concept of free trade is, admittedly, an issue that resonates more with the financial and political world's elites on the coasts than with regular people in the heartland. To be sure, it is a tragedy when anyone loses a job. But the question too few in the media are asking is whether society as a whole would be better off if America decided to retreat from the global economy and employ its resources in unproductive industries in which it had no competitive advantage. Wouldn't these insular economic policies eventually increase costs for all American consumers, limiting the ability of firms to increase their profits, and eventually limit their ability to hire workers?

To rail against free trade is essentially to take on the precepts of classical economics upon which America was based. Adam Smith spoke presciently about these issues more than 200 years ago. He and the other classical economists that followed him believed that government interference in the economy should be held to a minimum (often referred to as laissez-faire capitalism) and that free trade would lead to the most efficient use of the world's resources, and thus maximize world welfare.[9]

Fortunately, there are a number of thoughtful commentators who have started to spread the gospel of the benefits of free trade. Regular *New York Times* columnist Tom Friedman is one of the few who has written about the benefits of outsourcing:

> **Consider one of the newest products to be outsourced to India: animation. Yes, a lot of your Saturday morning cartoons are drawn by Indian animators like JadooWorks, founded three years ago here in Bangalore.... India, though, did not take these basic animation jobs from Americans. For 20 years they had been outsourced by U.S. movie companies, first to Japan and then to the Philippines, Korea, Hong Kong, and Taiwan. The sophisticated, and more lucrative, pre-production, finishing, and marketing of the animated films, though, always remained in America. Indian animation companies took business away from the other Asians by proving to be more adept at both the hand-drawing of characters and the digital painting of each frame by computer—at a lower price. But here is where the story really gets interesting. JadooWorks has decided to produce its own animated feature on the childhood of Krishna. To write the script, though, it wanted the best storyteller it could find, and outsourced the project to an Emmy Award–winning U.S. animation writer, Jeffrey Scott—for an Indian epic! ... All of the voices are done with American actors in L.A., and the music is written in London. JadooWorks also creates computer games for the global market but outsources all the game concepts to U.S. and British game designers. All the computers and animation software are imported from America (HP and IBM) or Canada.** [10]

Even some of the government's own data suggests that more jobs are *insourced* to the United States than are outsourced outside its borders. Using data from the U.S. Department of Commerce, the dollar value of American *exports* of legal services, computer programming, telecommunications, financial services, engineering, management consulting, and other private services rose sharply in 2003 to $131 billion.

U.S. imports of these services also rose, but only stood at $77 billion for the year. That is to say, America insources nearly $53 billion more in such services than it outsources. Although some might say that phenomenon is only occurring in the service industries and thus ignores the difficulties in the manufacturing sector, it is important to remember that only 20 percent of the U.S. economy is in manufacturing.

Many of the same fears about U.S. job losses existed with Japan's emergence in the 1970s and 1980s. Remarkably, nearly 20 years later, Japan's competitive advantages in the auto industry have allowed it to build plants and hire workers in the United States. Says legendary banker Walter Wriston:

> **We are importing many more jobs than we export. Indeed foreign companies of all kinds from all over the word are attracted to our stable political environment, our relatively low corporate tax rate, and the huge growth in productivity by American workers. Many foreign companies trying to compete in the global market carry the cost of residual socialism found in some European countries, and they look to the U.S. as a far more salubrious business climate.**[11]

Ironically, the media's fascination with the concept of outsourcing began just as the unemployment rate in the United States started to decline (see Chart 5-2). Largely absent from the discussion of the economy in this election year is the fact that the unemployment rate has been falling and as of June 2004 was at 5.6 percent, below the 6 percent rate generally considered consistent with full employment before the late 1990s bubble. The impact of free trade and labor

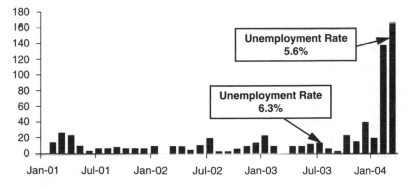

CHART 5-2 "Outsourcing" Index: Number of Instances the Phrase Appears in the *New York Times*

markets may create greater job insecurity in the short term, but it is important to remember that in the long term such policies boost corporate profits and long-term employment prospects.

A New Industrial Revolution: Information Technology

Faced with increasing competitive pressures from both home and abroad, today's companies are not only seeking cheaper labor from abroad, but are also looking for ways to dramatically cut costs through technology at home. The implications of the increasingly central role technology is occupying in commerce are wide-ranging, but its most important impact has been on productivity and cost.

The benefits of technology on productivity accrue to all companies in our economy—labor versus capital intensive, domestic versus multinational, and old versus new. Nowhere has the technology-related surge in productivity been more apparent than in retailing, where volume per worker is 35 percent greater today than it was a mere five years ago. Even cutting-edge "new economy" Cisco boosted its Internet-related savings from $650 million in 1999 to $2.1 billion in 2003.[12]

There is perhaps no concept that better exemplifies the power of technology on productivity and efficiency than "Moore's Law." First put forth by one of the original founders of Intel, Gordon Moore, in the 1970s, "Moore's Law" held that semiconductors would halve in price or double in power every 18 months. While Moore believed that this acceleration in computing capacity would start to wane by the mid-1980s, the massive increase in the speed of computer chips and the decline in their cost has continued to this day. As Brian Wesbury, chief economist of investment bank Griffin, Kubik, Stephens & Thompson points out in *The New Era of Wealth*, "By 1998, microchip prices had fallen to just 1 percent of their cost in 1980. If automobile prices had followed the same path, a $20,000 car in 1980 would cost just $200 today."[13]

It is important to note that the term "technology" is only a substitute for the term "innovation." For example, the latest developments in the financial markets, with regard to new financial products and increased access to the world's capital markets, are a form of technological innovation. At the very least, the deregulation and the democratization of the world's capital markets have allowed innovators in all industries greater opportunities than ever before to put their ideas to work.

Because technology may be the American worker's only real protection against the vast pool of cheap labor existing outside its shores, it would again be a mistake to assume that the new challenges of technology will ultimately damage employment opportunities for American workers. Technology may indeed eliminate the need for certain jobs, but it is important to remember that it creates new ones. In much the same way, free trade and globalization create opportunities for American workers, technology and innovation—in manufacturing, in financial services, and the flow of information—has clearly become America's chief competitive advantage in the global economy, raising the living standards of all of its citizens. Indeed, technology has become an increasingly large part of our economy.

If there were any doubts that technology and intellectual capital lay at the heart of the U.S. economy, a quick look at the country's balance of trade would put them to rest. In 1999, when there were few anxieties about the country's economic might, America's chief "exports" were the licensing fees and royalties it collected from abroad, easily surpassing foreign sales of aircraft, its chief physical export.[14]

While anxieties have risen substantially about the impact of technology on employment in recent years, recent job gains suggest that these fears are overblown. Bruce Nussbaum of *BusinessWeek* put it this way: "While America's faith in its innovation economy has often been tested, it has never been betrayed. Given the chance, the economy will deliver the jobs and prosperity it has in the past."[15]

Investing in Creative Destruction

Economist Joseph A. Schumpeter deemed the virtues of the new global economy described in the preceding pages as the process of "creative destruction." In his classic, *Capitalism, Socialism, and Democracy,* Schumpeter argued that free markets and ever-greater levels of competition actually *increase* aggregate living standards. He writes:

> **[the] opening of new markets, foreign or domestic ... revolutionizes the economic structure from within, incessantly destroying the old one, incessantly creating a new one. This process of Creative Destruction is the essential fact about capitalism. It is what capitalism consists in and what every capitalist concern has got to live in.**[16]

For investors, it is important to remember that with the increasingly fast paced nature of global commerce, it may mean that only the best companies will prosper. In the absence of products, services, or processes that are truly unique, technological innovation and global competition will mean that competitive advantages in most industries will be worn away quickly. Investors should also remember that these threats won't always come from abroad either. Companies like Sears and Montgomery Ward learned the hard way that the most potent threats can come from your own backyard. Remarkably, the internal positioning documents of Sears didn't even mention Wal-Mart until the 1980s.[17]

Freer access to capital has only increased the competitive nature of the global economy, affording small companies the ability to compete with large ones more easily. This probably means more volatility, more disparate outcomes among companies, and lower aggregate returns. For equity investors, it also requires greater vigilance in monitoring their holdings.

Key Take-Aways

1. Free trade, globalization, and technology are secular forces that are making the global economy increasingly competitive and are changing the social contract between corporations and their employees.
2. Free trade may mean greater insecurity for American workers in the short term, but it also means larger foreign markets for American companies in the long term.
3. The China Miracle is for real. The supply of cheap labor and the rapidly expanding productive capacity will continue to make China an engine for both global growth and disinflation.
4. Fears over outsourcing are overblown—government data suggest that more jobs are insourced to the U.S. than outsourced out its borders.
5. The effective use of technology boosts productivity, lowers costs, and increases profits. While technological innovation may eliminate jobs, it also creates new ones.
6. Companies that harness the opportunities presented by free trade and technology will outperform those that do not, by a wide margin.
7. The potential for more rapidly changing fortunes of American companies will require investors to be more conscientious about their equity holdings.

Part II

≈

A Framework for Investing

6

TAKING ADVANTAGE OF THE CHANGES IN INVESTMENT RESEARCH

OPPORTUNITIES AND PITFALLS IN A POST-BUBBLE ENVIRONMENT

Never play poker with a man named Doc.
Never eat in a restaurant called Mom's.
Never sleep with a woman who's got more troubles
than you.

NELSON ALGREN

CRITICISM OF BROKERAGE HOUSE (sell-side) research is nothing new. Fred Schwed put it this way in *Where Are the Customers Yachts?*, which is perhaps one of the funniest books ever written about Wall Street, published in 1940 and reprinted recently:

> The statisticians are housed way down the hall in scholarly quiet. No noisy tickers or loquacious customers are allowed to intrude, and the Thinkers are surrounded by tomes of reference and the latest news flashes from everywhere. They all carry slide rules, which as everyone knows are more scientific than divining rods. They make exhaustive studies of many a "special situation" and eventually get to know absolutely everything about the affairs of a certain corporation, except perhaps one detail, which is shortly after the inception of the ensuing fiscal year, the corporation is going into [bankruptcy].[1]

Working with Jim Moltz, Ed Hyman, and Nancy Lazar, I've often heard about the good old days on Wall Street when being a research analyst actually had some cachet. The old crew from the predecessor to my firm, C.J. Lawrence, was considered to be one the best at providing thought-provoking and independent research in an era where such analysis was more readily available and, in many ways, more sought after.

After three years in the desert of a bear market, I started to wonder about how our business had lost its way. I then picked up a piece last summer from C.J.'s old oil analyst, the redoubtable Charley Maxwell. The brief four-page report on the state of the oil market in 2004 and beyond spoke volumes about the way Street research had changed throughout the years.

A former "rabbit" for legendary miler Roger Bannister, and whose dire warnings to the auto industry in the '70s were recounted in David Halberstam's *The Reckoning,* Charley has always been talked about with respect and, often, humor in our shop and on the Street. But while his study and his conclusions were impressive as usual, it was the style that struck me. No fancy jargon. No fancy font. No table pounding. In essence, just good, solid information presented in an humble way. Charley wasn't trying to sell you anything. He was trying to educate you. This was, I thought, the most significant way in which the Street had changed. His piece got me to think about the present state and the future of sell-side research in an environment of greater regulation and lower commissions. It also made me wonder about how we got into this mess and how we can get out of it.

May Day and the Collapse of Independent Research

To understand how Street research had come to earn its present reputation, one first needs to understand its roots. While the financial press has picked up on the concept of independent research with a thrill of discovery in recent years, there were once scores of independent firms like ISI and C.J. Lawrence on the Street. It might be hard to believe, but before the dawn of negotiated commissions, there were hundreds of firms providing in-depth and objective research without being tainted by the influence of the firm's investment banking relationships.

Before "May Day," as it was affectionately called at the time, brokers charged minimum fixed commissions on buy and sell orders. Needless to say, those commissions were fixed at high (some say exorbitant) rates. Given the fact that set prices made investors indifferent to doing their business with one broker over another, hundreds of regional and independent research firms prospered. By all accounts, the 1960s and early 1970s was a great time to be in the brokerage business. With fixed commissions, one old-timer told me that this was the golden age of travel and entertainment: "Limousine services lined the block around Madison Square Garden waiting to take brokers and their clients home."

But that all changed on May 1, 1975, when fixed commissions, a practice in place since the Buttonwood Tree Agreement establishing the New York Stock Exchange in 1792, were eliminated. For many brokers, this reform had been viewed with dread since the advent of the over-the-counter market, Nasdaq, in 1971. NYSE member firms had argued strenuously against this reform, believing it would hurt already weakened profitability from greater operations needs, make institutional research less readily available, irrevocably damage the national distribution system of strong regional firms, and ultimately result in higher commissions for the small investor.[2] One member firm predicted that May Day would result in the failure of as many as 200 regional brokers and independent research firms. While many saw this as an exaggeration, the estimate proved to be on the low side.[3]

Almost immediately, institutional commission rates fell 40 percent and brokers began sorting themselves into discount brokers offering low commissions and limited services, and "full service" brokers offering a wide range of products for commission rates not far from the old rates.[4] While volume surged, negotiated commissions forced many research boutiques like William D. Witter, R.W. Pressprich & Company, and Mitchell, Hutchins & Company to reinvent themselves, at best, and close their doors, at worst.

The first such firm to go under in the wake of negotiated rates was Auerback, Pollack & Richardson, which announced that it was closing its doors for good on September 29, 1975. *Institutional Investor* called the firm "a sort of research Camelot, a symbol of all that was best about the firms that raised the pursuit of investment ideas to unprecedented, if costly, heights."[5] Wainwright & Company, with its comprehensive 50-page company reports, was another example of this golden age of independent research. It, too, was forced to close its doors. Claimed Chris Welles in *The Last Days of the Club*, his book on the last days of negotiated commissions in 1975, "There are probably more individuals and firms involved in research than any other single function on Wall Street."[6]

The shuttering of firms like Auerbeck and Wainwright sent a powerful message to Wall Street power brokers—investment research was, in and of itself, an unprofitable business—and marked a new era in which the full service firm relied on trading rather than research to drive profits. Even five years after May Day, research commissions were Wall Street's largest revenue source, accounting for 35 percent of total revenues. By 1990 research generated commissions were only 16 percent of the total. Merger and acquisition activity, on the other hand, rose from 13 percent of Wall Street revenues in 1980 to 32 percent in 1990.[7]

Slowly but surely, the relationship between investment banking and investment research then became cozier, chipping away at the vaunted "Chinese Wall" that was supposed to eliminate such conflicts of interest. While the end of fixed commissions allowed volume to rise and increased competition among brokers, in hindsight one must wonder whether an unintended consequence of May Day was to actually hurt those it had been most intended to help. Indeed, the irony of lower commissions was that they encouraged more individuals to buy stocks while at the same time providing the impetus for the slow and steady decline in the quality and usefulness of Wall Street research. In essence, many customers were getting what they paid for. And for many investors, this was when sell-side research added the most value.

Decline in Quality, Eliot Spitzer, and the Settlement

In the old days, good analysts were thought of as people who would hit the road, not to visit their institutional clients, per se, but to visit managements and suppliers and to kick a few tires. Perhaps not exactly green eyeshade types, but certainly a far cry from the über-salesman and media darlings they would become a generation later.

Perhaps one of the best examples of what research was all about in those days is Martin Sass's call on television manufacturers in the 1960s. As recounted in Ron Insana's *Traders' Tales*, Sass, later to become one of the Street's experts on distressed securities, was then a junior analyst for Argus Research. On his way to visit management, Sass learned that his taxi driver was an idled employee of the preeminent manufacturer of color televisions at the time, Motorola, and that the company was sitting on a ton of inventory. Unable to gain meaningful insights from the company itself, Sass decided to talk to more laid-off workers at a local watering hole near the plant. They confirmed the taxi driver's story, and upon his return to New York, Sass issued "sell" recommendations on the industry group. He was later vindicated when the Japanese overtook the United States in the manufacture of color television sets.[8]

Unfortunately, after May Day such stories were rare, and sell-side research went on its merry way, growing in influence and self-importance with the bull market that started in 1982. The quality of research began to decline little by little, with directors of research becoming more beholden to other parts of the investment banks that employed them. The conflicts between research and the corporate finance departments became so prevalent, in fact, that most simply accepted the fact that, by July 2000, less than 1 percent of the 28,000 individual analyst recommendations were sells and strong sells, while more than 66 percent were either buys or strong buys.[9] As an example, Jack Grubman, star telecom analyst for Citigroup, and later immortalized by the financial media for his role in the WorldCom scandal, covered 34 companies and had buy recommendations on all but three. Mary Meeker, another bubble baby, known as the "Queen of the Internet," had recommendations of "outperform" on all but two of the 20 companies she covered.[10]

Everyone knew the game, of course, but no one much minded when stocks continued to go up. It was only after stocks peaked in March 2000 that people started asking questions and the atmosphere turned ugly. There was perhaps no greater symbol of the growing public anger about the role of sell-side analysts in the creation of the bubble than CNBC's ambush interview of fallen star telecom analyst Jack Grubman outside the Metropolitan Museum of Art.

Among most people on my side of the Street, there was incredulousness that what we did was important enough to make a reporter (from CNBC, no less) wish to act out his Mike Wallace fantasy. We wrote dry reports, created mind-numbing earnings models, and took the 5:30 a.m. flight to Des Moines. This wasn't Abscam (the name derived from a fictitious company the FBI set up to lure various public officials into accepting bribes)—or was it? Some of us on the sellside watched the scene with a sense of *schadenfreude*, while others, like myself, watched with a sense of dread. Ever the providers of sympathy in our shop, one of the bond salesmen turned to me after this episode and said, "I would start wearing a hat and sunglasses if I were you. When this is all over, they're going to hunt down equity strategists like wildebeest." On that day, I wasn't so sure he was wrong.

Of course, when the public and the media start to turn on an industry, the country's regulatory machinery can't be too far behind. Chief among the public interrogators was, of course, New York Attorney General Eliot Spitzer. Using an obscure state law called the Martin Act, Spitzer employed the full power of his office to charge Wall Street firms with civil and criminal fraud violations. The crux of Spitzer's indictment of a system that had existed for more than two decades came from what would have once been considered unlikely sources: Merrill Lynch Internet analyst Henry Blodget and the aforementioned Jack Grubman. A former journalist, Blodget's only real claim to fame prior to his employment contract with Merrill was that he was the most bullish of all the analysts covering Amazon, perhaps the most sought-after investment banking relationship in the world at the time.

Investigating alleged abuses on Wall Street, Attorney General Spitzer subpoenaed the various e-mails of Merrill's analysts and investment bankers. The cynicism and classlessness of these e-mails surprised even the most hardened of Wall Street veterans, but they clearly highlighted what many had believed for some time: Analysts often held far more negative opinions about the stocks they covered than was revealed in their public statements and research reports. The once high-flying Internet company Infospace, for example, was on Merrill's 15 Most Favored list despite the fact that Blodget described the company as a "powder keg." In another example, Grubman maintained a buy recommendation on Focal, despite the fact that he said privately that it should be rated "underperform." These incriminating e-mails gave the attorney general the opening he needed to set off a series of reforms more comprehensive than anything seen since the 1930s.

The eventual result of Spitzer's investigations was a $1.4 billion omnibus settlement with 14 of Wall Street's largest investment banks, signed late in 2002. The country's largest banks agreed to pay $900 million in fines, $450 million to pay for independent research, and $85 million for "investor education." The reforms set forth in the agreement barred sell-side analysts from being paid from the corporate finance arms of their firms and banned them from accompanying investment bankers on pitches to prospective clients and road shows for initial public offerings and secondaries. Blodget and Grubman were both forced to pay heavy fines and were subjected to lifetime bans from the security industry.

As a result, investment banks are now taking a far more careful and modest approach to investment research. According to Joe Gatto,

CEO of StarMine, an independent arbiter of analyst performance, the number of analysts' recommendations (as measured by analyst-security pairs with new recommendations in the prior 30 days) has remained fairly constant, in the 3,000 to 4,000 range from 1998 to today, although the analyst headcounts are down about 20 percent on average at the top 20 firms. But there has been an increase, however slight, in the number of strong sells, sells, and holds analysts are willing to put on the stocks they cover (see Chart 6-1). Certainly, the salaries of research analysts are far lower these days, and the number of companies banks are willing to cover has fallen markedly. Sadly, the result has been an increase in the cost of capital for companies in smaller industries that don't generate large commissions.

Sell-Side Research and Performance

Of course, questioning Street research's contribution to investment performance is nothing new. Burton Malkiel devoted an entire chapter to the "incompetence" of research analysis in his seminal work, *A Random Walk Down Wall Street*, in 1973. But the major difference between the skepticism of Malkiel then and the widespread pessimism about the state of the profession now was a question of motive.

In the early 1970s, Malkiel didn't spend much time wondering whether analysts' research was tainted by the desire to curry favor with potential investment banking clients, he merely wondered whether anyone could add value to the investment process if the markets were truly efficient. This concern didn't go away in the 1980s and '90s, but new anxieties emerged with the very public escapades of Grubman, Blodget, Mary Meeker, and others. Certainly, the Spitzer

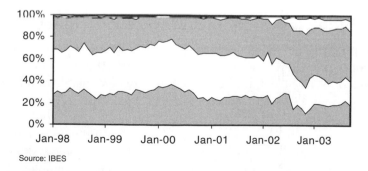

Source: IBES

CHART 6-1   Distribution of New Analyst Recommendations

era has provided wide-ranging reforms among sell-side analysts. But the question still remains: Are sell-side earnings estimates and buy-sell-hold recommendations good leading or contrary indicators?

An article in *Investor's Business Daily* entitled "Analysts Make Calls, but Market Doesn't Listen" tried to find the answer to this question and commissioned Zacks to gauge the performance of the most and least recommended stocks from 1999 to 2003. Starting with a universe of 3,000 analyst-covered stocks trading at $10 a share or higher, *IBD* found that the 600 *most-recommended* stocks, based on a weighting of analyst ratings, lost 24 percent in 2000, 5.1 percent in 2001, and 20.7 percent in 2002, while rising 20.7 percent through July 2003. While this is surprising, it was the performance of the *least-recommended* stocks in that stretch that was most shocking: In stark contrast, the 600 least-recommended rose 6.4 percent in 2000 and 20.5 percent in 2001, fell 16.4 percent in 2002, and rose more than 35 percent through July 2003, trouncing their most-recommended rivals four years running.[11]

It's difficult to gloss over these findings. Even the most resolute skeptic would find it difficult to claim that Street research in the aggregate stands as a good contrarian indicator. But while the poor predictive qualities of Street research is more than a little surprising, *IBD*'s study should allow the prudent investor to use Street recommendations to their advantage. To this end, I regularly employ the computing capabilities of FactSet, using data from FirstCall, to determine which stocks are currently the most or least recommended by the Street. FirstCall assigns a *1* to stocks with highest rankings (strong buys) and a *5* to stocks with the lowest rankings (strong sells). It then averages all of the analysts' individual calls to come up with the stock's average rating.

Sell-Side Research and Market Efficiency

If the poor predictive qualities of sell-side research weren't enough to convince you there's something wrong with the current research process on Wall Street, the relationship between volatility and analyst coverage may be even more compelling. In a truly efficient market where analysts provided "value added" research, one would assume that depth of sell-side coverage would quickly eliminate pricing inefficiencies and misperceptions. And yet, as the table below shows, the volatility of the six largest and most widely followed technology stocks is 50 percent higher than the largest stocks in the relatively underfol-

TABLE 6-1   Analyst Coverage: Industrials vs. Technology, Top Six by Market Cap

SECTOR	COMPANY	MARKET CAP*	SELL-SIDE COVERAGE	BETA
Industrials	General Electric	$289,043.7	19.0	1.2
	United Parcel Service	$76,151.3	21.0	0.5
	3M	$57,707.5	18.0	0.7
	Tyco International	$43,741.4	13.0	0.8
	United Technologies	$39,171.6	22.0	1.1
	Caterpillar	$32,074.2	17.0	1.2
	Average	**$89,648.3**	**18**	**0.92**
Technology	Microsoft	$313,113.0	34.0	1.2
	Intel	$206,757.6	32.0	1.8
	IBM	$160,457.0	20.0	1.2
	Cisco Systems	$147,098.0	46.0	1.5
	Dell	$93,090.0	27.0	1.1
	Hewlett-Packard	$66,834.1	20.0	1.6
	Average	**$164,558.3**	**30**	**1.39**

*In hundreds of dollars

lowed Industrials sector. The obvious conclusion is that sell-side research creates more questions than it answers.

Case Study: Taiwan

While the revelations about the complicity of sell-side analysts in the scandals that rocked Wall Street in the wake of the bubble are shocking, the vast majority of analysts are honest, hardworking people who try to "call 'em as they see 'em" under constant pressure from their employers, their clients, and the companies they cover. For most of us on the sell-side, New York Attorney General Eliot Spitzer's regular appearances on CNBC last year became about as welcome as an American Express bill after Christmas. But in some respects, sell-side analysts should be thankful that we only have Mr. Spitzer to contend with.

After a brutal bear market and a wide-ranging financial scandal of one of its largest companies (the Cathay Group Ponzi scheme), Taiwan actually took the unprecedented step of outlawing sell-side research altogether in the 1980s. Eerily reminiscent of what would occur in America two decades later, Taiwanese brokerage firms would load up on stocks, write highly promotional research reports on them, and then dump the shares on an unsuspecting public as the stocks rose.[12]

Recognizing that the country needed vibrant capital markets to provide economic growth and attract foreign capital, Taiwan's Ministry of Finance then decided to let foreign investors develop the research industry. Although foreigners had been previously barred from investing in Taiwanese shares, Fidelity Investments, under the direction of John Vail, established its Taiwan Fund in Taipei to serve the dual purpose of attracting foreign capital and training home-grown investment research analysts in Western buy-side equity research techniques. Because there were no longer any financial ana-lysts, Fidelity went out and hired bank credit analysts. Eventually, Taiwan once again allowed brokerage firms to publish sell-side research reports under strict new ethical guidelines. By all accounts, the quality of research improved. But American brokerage firms and securities' industry regulators should take little solace in this example, for what happened next was truly amazing.

As John Vail describes it:

> Soon after our arrival, Taiwan entered a bubble that made all others look puny. The index rose from 600 to 12,000 by early 1990. Foreigners were allowed to enter the brokerage industry, so the quality of sell-side research improved, but such did not matter greatly, as trading became dominated by taxi drivers and housewives. At one textile company I was visiting, the CEO told me that he had to install a phone bank for factory workers and give them a 10 minute break every hour in order for them to trade. Otherwise, he said, they would quit and join the others in the brokerage retail trading rooms.[13]

What lessons can be drawn from this episode? For brokerage firms, the Taiwan example in the 1980s and their own experiences in the United States in recent years should serve as painful reminders that research needs to be truly independent if it is to have any worth at all. It should also be an indication of how far regulators can and will go if they believe brokerage firms haven't fully gotten the message. Outlawing sell-side research might make American investors more cautious in their investments, but it would also severely limit our econ-omy's ability to raise capital for new companies and new technologies.

Taiwan's experience with tainted sell-side research and its own efforts to improve it should also give regulators pause. As the bubble in Taiwanese stocks after the introduction of improved and more ethically based research indicates, regulators can outlaw everything that might give rise to securities fraud except one: greed. While it is obvious that certain legal and ethical safeguards need to exist to protect investors from potential brokerage firm improprieties, it should be remembered that the ultimate responsibility for losses lies within.

A New Approach to Investment Research

Of course, bringing up problems is a lot easier than offering solutions. Outlawing sell-side research feels broadly anti-American. And while there are few easy answers to "fix" the problem of sell-side research, it seems clear that a more open discussion of the challenges facing analysts and brokerage firms is necessary. Certainly, a more thoughtful solution than the one offered by Attorney General Eliot Spitzer would go a long way in improving the stock selection process among institutional and retail investors alike. There may be no magic bullet, but there are a number of ways in which both the buy-side and sell-side could improve their investment research efforts:

Greater Emphasis on Nontraditional Research

Perhaps the best and most obvious improvement would come from analysts focusing on primary sources, in much the same way that ISI conducts its company surveys, rather than on the investor relations department. Byron Wien of Morgan Stanley once told me that, as a young tech analyst he learned more about what was happening at Hewlett Packard by sitting at the bar in a Palo Alto watering hole than he did by spending time at "official" meetings with company insiders. While that type of primary research hasn't been part of the program for some time, there are some hopeful signs that the sell-side is getting the message.

A short but interesting piece in the *Wall Street Journal* last fall recounted the story of an analyst at Bank of America who wound up calling a local police station to track down a company's claim that they would miss their quarterly earnings estimates because a high-margin shipment was involved in a freak traffic accident. The analyst claimed that the police videotapes of the accident suggested that the truck was nearly empty. At the very least, the analyst noted, such a large shipment on the last day of the quarter raised a serious "yellow flag."[14] His assessment was later vindicated.

More Self-Reliance, Hard Work, and Skepticism

Although virtually all Wall Street analysts and market pundits can talk a good enough game to dissuade the average investor from thinking he or she might be able to compete in the investment game, the truth of the matter is that Wall Street "expertise" is more often the result of hard work than intelligence or training. It was effort, for example, rather than the ability to tear apart a balance sheet, that was the distinguishing factor for the Bank of America analyst whose story was recounted above.

When it comes to investing in stocks, no amount of intelligence or education can take the place of the hours necessary to check on the status of a company's competitors and suppliers. While this may be discomfiting to those with outsized opinions of their own investment acumen, it should also be reassuring for the rest of us. The hours spent researching investments is the great equalizer. Certainly, if there were any doubts about the sell-side research process left, retail and institutional investors should realize the enormous pressures put on sell-side analysts by their employers, their clients, and the companies they cover and employ a greater degree of skepticism when sifting through analyst recommendations. Realizing, for instance, that the term "hold" has become the new "sell" recommendation on the Street, as we saw earlier in the chapter, should allow potential investors to look at research reports with an unjaundiced eye.

Sell-Side Analyst Box Scores

While few would disagree that primary in-depth research would go a long way in improving the investment process, it could be that sunshine is the best disinfectant for the conflicts inherent in brokerage house research. Throughout the year, Wall Street pays attention to analyst rankings from a variety of sources. But while these rankings provide some guide to the best analysts on Wall Street, they sometimes come up short because they fail to provide a worst-to-first list of the analysts in each category. Recognizing only the best analysts doesn't ensure the kind of accountability necessary for analysts to stand up for themselves and give their most objective analysis.

Of course, this is easy for me to say because I'm a strategist and often not held to the same standard as stock analysts. (We've been so discredited as a species that no one expects anything from us anyway.) But providing regular and publicly available "batting statistics" on sell-side analysts would become a must-read among investment professionals, and it would serve a useful public service by allowing retail and institutional investors alike to independently verify whether the reports they read are objective or paid for by investment banking.

One of the positive effects of the scandals on Wall Street is that new businesses have been created to increase the transparency of the basic building blocks of an investment decision: financial statements and brokerage analyst research. One such firm, StarMine, has started to use the historical record of brokerage analyst recommendations and earnings estimates to rank the effectiveness of sell-side analysts. This information has been important for both brokerage firms and institutional investors in determining the true value of broker research, and it has proved effective in isolating those companies most likely to post earnings surprises.[15]

As you might imagine, this suggestion has not exactly endeared me to my sell-side colleagues. But being a big fan of my profession (the prospect of doing anything else for a living is too frightening for me to contemplate), I believe, paraphrasing Tancredi in the epic Italian novel *The Leopard*, that "if we want things to stay as they are, they will have to change." When hearing this suggestion, a number of sell-side analysts have pointed out, not altogether incorrectly, that the buy-side doesn't really rely on sell-side recommendations when making their investment decisions, but rather, uses the sell-side for idea generation and as a means of testing their own investment theses. This is at least in part true. But to merely leave the discussion here would disregard the needs of the retail investor and create greater questions about the importance of research altogether.

One might argue that if individual stock recommendations were as useless as some have suggested, sell-side analysts shouldn't make any recommendations at all. Unfortunately, believing that sell-side analysts shouldn't be subject to the same type of objective performance analysis to which our institutional clients are beholden allows us as a profession to take credit for our good calls while shirking responsibility for our bad ones. This, in turn, damages our credibility and invites greater regulatory scrutiny.

Analyst box scores would allow the sell-side and buy-side alike to more easily determine the value of the brokerage house research. Greater transparency will do more to restore investor confidence than any host of new laws could conceivably provide.

Retail Investor Education

I once read that when Las Vegas casinos first started to operate, managements forbade hotel gift shops from selling books on gambling. In theory, better gamblers would hurt the casino's bottom line. Over time, however, forward-looking casino executives realized that better informed gamblers enjoyed their experience more, were more apt to come back, and all in all were far better customers. Today, bettors can find a small library on virtually every game of chance in the gift shop of any self-respecting casino.

In much the same way, Wall Street needs to start acting on its promise to treat its customers as partners rather than a short-term ticket to commissions. Fortunately, most major brokerage firms have begun to emphasize asset gathering rather than heavy account turnover when compensating their brokers.

Public Company Accountability

While the media has often put the onus on brokerage house analysts to ferret out fundamental changes in the companies they cover, few have emphasized the responsibility of public companies in helping brokerage firms provide quality research.

Many public companies have not been shy in seeking retribution against analysts that were unwilling to toe the company line. At the beginning of the end of the great '90s bull market, it was not unheard of for companies to lock out analysts who issued downgrades or negative comments on their stock from conference calls and meetings with management. Sadly, in an effort to maintain their investment banking relationships, many brokerage firms and research directors felt compelled to back down from such confrontations. John Vail suggested that public companies who utilized such tactics against research analysts should be placed on a public list maintained by the CFA Institute, the official organization of the Chartered Financial Analyst designation. Indeed, in this era of greater regulatory scrutiny and civil litigation, the specter of being placed on that list would provide a significant deterrent to strong-arm tactics designed to obfuscate the truth.

Ultimately, all the above suggestions drive at two fundamental approaches to improving investment research: transparency and accountability. Publicly available metrics of the effectiveness of sell research and the willingness of public companies to work with the investment community would go a long way in removing a number of conflicts that led to the egregious abuses of the late 1990s. Furthermore, both buy-side and sell-side analysts will be well served to dig deeper than the information that is so generously provided to them. Greater self-reliance and a greater reliance on nontraditional sources of information will undoubtedly improve the quality of investment research.

Key Take-Aways

1. The advent of negotiated commissions had the unintended consequence of limiting independent research.
2. Evidence suggests that traditional sell-side research is actually a good contrarian indicator.
3. Investors will be well-served to utilize nontraditional sources of research and to be more self-reliant in the years to come.
4. Sell-side box scores will provide a major incentive for brokerage firms to eliminate potential conflicts of interest.

7

THE NEED FOR A NEW CONTRARIAN APPROACH

CHARTING YOUR OWN PATH

"It ain't what you don't know that gets you in trouble. It's what you know for sure that just ain't so."

—MARK TWAIN

Ask ANY NOVICE GAMBLER what the object of the game blackjack is and they'll tell you that it's "to get 21." But ask any professional gambler the same question and he'll say simply "to beat the dealer." At once obvious and illuminating, many investors come up short in their portfolios for one simple reason—they don't know the object of the game they're playing.

Nowhere is this more obvious than in the concept of contrarian investing—the insight, and courage, to buy when everyone else is selling, and sell when everyone else is buying.

When I spend time with retail investors at conferences or with young research analysts and salesmen on the Street, the concept of getting excited about stocks everyone else hates, and being skeptical about stocks everyone else loves, can be foreign and uncomfortable. But it is this concept, in practice, that sets the truly great investors apart from the also-rans. While any professional investor worth his salt believes strongly in the power of measured contrarianism, only the very best investors use the concept effectively enough to boost performance. In this chapter we will discuss the origins of contrarian investment strategies and why they work, new methods for determining when the consensus is overly bullish or overly bearish, and finally, why it's more important to make money than to be "smart."

The Contrarian Approach in a Nutshell

One of central ironies of the explosion of financial news and media outlets over the last few years has been that investors, who now have access to a voluminous amount of information on the economy and public companies, appear more confused about their investments than ever before.

In the year 2000, for example, despite almost instantaneous access to the news, both professional and individual investors alike missed the mark badly after the bubble burst. As we have seen in the chapters about sell-side research and corporate responsibility, there is little doubt that unscrupulous Wall Street analysts and corporate chieftains are at least partly to blame for the market's dramatic decline in the wake of the Internet bubble. But not enough has been written about the complicity of the media in exacerbating the volatility of financial markets and creating an environment in which investors of all stripes became susceptible to the "group think" that so often results in disastrous investment (and for that matter, personal) decisions.

Of course, societal norms have conditioned us to believe that there is "safety in numbers," that what seems to be accepted knowledge is in fact true. While this may be a helpful mind-set while walking around in a foreign city, it can be harmful when it comes to investing. Why?

Simply stated, *when everyone is bearish, there are only potential buyers; when everyone is bullish, there are only potential sellers.* It is the *potential* for investors to buy, rather than the current level of buying interest, that creates value for the long-term investor.

When explaining this concept to people new to the market, I find it useful to ask them to think about the stock market as a fireplace with only five logs on a bitterly cold day. Few people might be interested in sitting next to this fireplace before a single log is placed on the fire, but that is precisely the time those wishing to stay warm for the longest period of time would seek a place by the hearth. On the other hand, almost everyone wants to get near the fire once it's burning, with all five logs ablaze. And that would be the time when those most interested in their personal comfort should start to look for other sources of warmth. In essence, the potential heat our fire will provide is greatest before a single log is placed on the fire.

This is instructive when investing in stocks. The fuel for any long-term investment (our fire) is the amount of capital (the number of logs) available to purchase it. Once that last log is placed on the fire, its ability to generate heat (returns) starts to diminish. In many ways this is precisely what happened in the Internet bubble of the late 1990s.

By March of 2000, with the Nasdaq at 5,000, there were scores of people who quit their day jobs to trade stocks. Hundreds of Web sites were established to help amateurs speculate, and online brokers were all too eager to provide access and financing to purchase stocks. It was great while it lasted, but only the most astute and courageous investors and market gurus recognized that the blaze that was the great bull market of the late 1990s was rapidly running out of fuel. Famed finance professor Jeremy Siegel of the Wharton School was one such guru, who penned "Big Cap Stocks Are a Sucker Bet" on the op-ed pages of the *Wall Street Journal* two weeks before the Nasdaq peaked in March 2000—in retrospect, one of the greatest short term calls on the stock market of all time.

The great bull market in Internet and tech-related shares lasted a lot longer than anyone could have predicted. But eventually the least likely buyer of stocks opened his account online in much the same way the last log is placed on a fire. At that stage of the game, there were only potential sellers, and the heat that the great bull market generated diminished little by little until it was all gone. Ultimately, investors need to remember that the potential return on any investment is the relationship of its current price to the discounted cash-flows of its income. *Purchasing shares in any company is a bet not on the present, but on the future.*

Lord Keynes: The First Contrarian

George Bernard Shaw supposedly once quipped, "If all economists were laid end to end, they would not reach a conclusion." Economists and other "experts" can be easy targets when it comes to investing. Time and again, throughout the market's history, many economists have distinguished themselves as being lackluster investors. Legendary economist Irving Fischer, noted for his early work on monetary theory, essentially cemented the reputation of economists as poor market forecasters when he claimed, just weeks before the Great Crash of 1929, that stocks had reached a "permanently high plateau."[1]

Although economists will likely never shake their reputation as poor investors, students of financial history would be well served to remember one notable and important exception—John Maynard Keynes, the father of post-Depression economics. While his theories about the relationship between government spending and the business cycle are well-known and have influenced Washington's economic policies to this day—sadly, in my opinion—it is Keynes's contrarian approach and his remarkable investment success that has set him apart from the scores of other academics, theoreticians, and market gurus who have held forth on the market.

Born the son of professors from Cambridge University, Keynes developed a fiercely independent approach to his study of the economy and the markets. Trained as a mathematician, and studying under the great Victorian economist Alfred Marshall, Keynes steadfastly refused to rely on the unrealistic assumptions that were so often the basis for economic theory, believing that economics was a branch of logic rather than a pseudonatural science.[2] Although Keynes started to speculate in the market by the age of 22, he did not become serious about investing until he was 36 years old.[3] It was only after winning and losing several fortunes that Keynes began to develop his trademark contrarian approach.

Upon leaving Her Majesty's Treasury in 1919, Keynes began to speculate in foreign exchange and was initially quite successful. But his victories were short-lived when, in 1920, extreme volatility in the currency market wiped out his assets and those entrusted to him by friends and family.[4] With no lack of confidence, he borrowed 5,000 pounds from financier Sir Ernest Cassel, obtained an advance on his upcoming book, *The Economic Consequences of Peace*, and delved deeper into the same positions that had been the source of his economic difficulty. By 1922, Keynes's net assets rebounded from a negative 8,587 to a positive 21,588 pounds.[5]

He refused to say that he had a set strategy, instead claiming that the overriding principle guiding his investments was "to go contrary to general opinion, on the ground that, if everyone is agreed about its merits, the investment is inevitably too dear and therefore unattractive."[6]

Despite his academic background and training, Keynes was almost entirely self-taught as an investor. His sophistication about what influences investors and the financial markets was impressive, even in relation to countless books that have been published on the subject over the last 70 years. His *General Theory of Employment, Interest, and Money* captured the essence of the game that had become Wall Street: "A conventional valuation that is established as the outcome of mass psychology of a large number of ignorant individuals is liable to change violently as the result of a sudden fluctuation of opinion due to factors that do not make much difference to the prospective yield; since there will be no roots of conviction to hold it steady."[7] Keynes recognized that most investors, whether professional or amateur, were "concerned, not with what an investment is really worth to a man who buys it for keeps. But with what the market will value it at, under the influence of mass psychology, three months or a year hence."[8] Sound familiar?

During the Great Depression, one of the most difficult periods ever in the annals of the global economy, Keynes was able to increase his net worth by 65 times.[9] In 1938, fresh from his investment success, he put forth the three investment principles that would become the basis for a whole new approach to investing in the financial markets:

1. A careful selection of a few investments (or a few types of investment) having regard to their cheapness in relation to their probable actual and potential *intrinsic* value over a period of years ahead, and in relation to alternative investments at the time.
2. A steadfast holding of these in fairly large units through thick and thin, perhaps for several years, until either they have fulfilled their promise or it is evident that they were purchased on a mistake.
3. A *balanced* investment position, i.e., a variety of risks in spite of individual holdings being large, and if possible opposed risks (e.g., a holding of gold shares among other equities, since they are likely to move in opposite directions when there are general fluctuations).[10]

Ultimately, Keynes's contrarian approach set him apart from the other economists and prognosticators of the time. At his death in 1945, he had amassed a fortune of about $20 million in 1993 dollars, a 25-year compound annual rate of return of better than 13 percent.[11] This is a truly remarkable record in a time when inflation was nonexistent. Keynes thus became the father of a new approach to investing—contrarianism. The aforementioned Irving Fischer, in contrast, went broke in the Great Crash and never recovered, having to borrow money from friends and relatives for the rest of his life.[12]

The Importance of Sentiment

While all professional money managers know that betting against the consensus at turning points is an important means of boosting returns, it is, of course, a lot easier said than done. Perhaps the most difficult part of contrarian investing is determining exactly where the consensus opinion lies. Many institutional money managers believe that a good strategist's main value rests with his ability to know how investors are positioned. But without the counsel of such "experts," where does one find information on the consensus opinion, or sentiment?

Even a cursory look at the weekly market magazine *Barron's*—a must read, incidentally, for anyone serious about investing—reveals that there are scores of statistics devoted to determining where the consensus opinion on stocks lies. Brokerage firms and letter writers have created literally hundreds of methods to gauge investor sentiment: the Arms Index, the Summary of Block Transactions, Investors Intelligence, Market Vane, *Barron's* Big Money Poll, the UBS Investor Sentiment Survey, New Highs and Lows, the Advance-Decline Line, the Put-Call Ratio, the VIX, and on and on. Because it's confusing even for someone who makes his living studying such minutiae, investors should develop a feel for a relatively limited number of indicators, knowing both their strengths and shortcomings.

Two types of sentiment indicators provide clues about the overall animal spirits of investors: *opinion-based indicators,* which often rely on surveys of individual and institutional investors, and market commentators; and *market-based indicators,* which determine sentiment simply by looking at the extent to which investors are making bullish or bearish bets on the market. Each has its place when attempting to determine how much investors have already discounted future expectations. But as we will see, market-based indicators are often far more effective at both indicating opportunity at market bottoms and risk at market tops.

Opinion-Based Indicators

Investors Intelligence

One of the most widely followed indicators of investor sentiment is provided by the Investors Intelligence company of New Rochelle, New York, which determines what percentage of 130 of investment advisers are bearish, bullish, or long-term bullish and expecting a short-term correction. When Investors Intelligence started its survey in 1963, Michael Burke and the other editors at the firm thought that the advisory services they polled would be able to pick market tops and bottoms. But to their surprise, they found that their survey was a good contrarian indicator because most market commentators were (and still are) trend followers. According to the company, when the number of bullish advisory firms climbs to more than 54 percent and the bears dip below 20 percent, it suggests that there are few buyers left to propel stocks further and that the market is therefore at risk.[13]

Market Vane, Barron's Big Money Poll, and UBS Investor Optimism

The Market Vane Corporation of Pasadena, California, also keeps track of sentiment stocks and a variety of other markets, like bonds and commodities, by tracking the buy and sell recommendations of leading market letter writers and commodity trading advisers.

Barron's, another valuable source, publishes the results of its Big Money Poll twice a year, which shows how institutional investors view the market. More detailed than other contrarian indicators, *Barron's* queries some of the biggest and most successful money managers about their opinions and not just on stocks, but also on their favorite sectors and their outlook on bonds and the Fed.

The UBS Index of Investor Optimism is also a survey, done in conjunction with the Gallup Organization. It queries 1,000 private investors who have over $10,000 of assets that can be invested. The survey did a great job of signaling excessive optimism in February 2000 and excessive pessimism in March 2003, as shown below in Chart 7-1.

The ISI Hedge Fund Survey

While all of the indicators listed above can be helpful at extremes, the proliferation of hedge funds and other speculative pools has lessened their effectiveness in recent years. Because hedge funds represent such a large portion of the Street's trading volume and commissions,

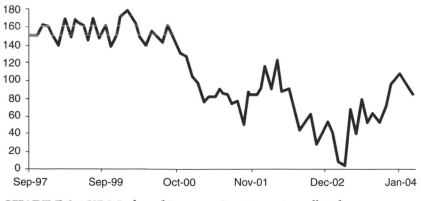

CHART 7-1 UBS Index of Investor Optimism: Overall Index

it has become increasingly dangerous to take the pulse of newsletter writers, traditional, institutional, or retail investors without also taking into account the sentiment of this new and crucial segment of the investment community. As far as I know, Oscar Sloterbeck and his team at ISI provide the only window into hedge fund sentiment on the Street by measuring both net exposure (long minus short positions) and gross exposure (long plus short positions).

At a little more than two years old, the jury is still out about the ISI survey's effectiveness over the long term. However, it was extremely effective at the depths of the bear market in 2003. By dropping to its nadir on March 5, 2003, only one week before the S&P low of 800.7 on March 11, the survey provided an important indication that stocks were oversold (see Chart 7-2), earning its place in the pantheon of our most important indicators. The S&P rose 39 percent and the Nasdaq rose 58 percent from the low through the end of 2003.

Market-Based Indicators

One of the standard raps against opinion-based sentiment indicators is that they are often far more effective at calling market bottoms than they are at calling market tops. While opinion-based indicators provide a quick and dirty window into the consensus, we have found that market-based indicators generally provide more consistent signals at both market tops and bottoms—because they rely on the markets themselves and represent the collective wisdom of the market's participants. Of course, it should be noted that investors can stay bullish

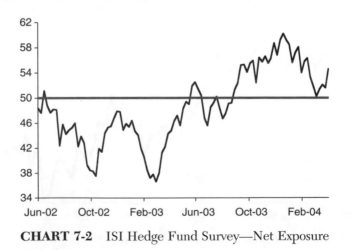

CHART 7-2   ISI Hedge Fund Survey—Net Exposure

a lot longer than the underlying fundamentals might justify, as we saw in the late 1990s.

Speculators and Wall Street strategists have created literally hundreds of measures of sentiment based on fund flows. It can be confusing, but we have found the indicators below to be most useful.

Short Interest

Every month the New York Stock Exchange, the Amex, and the National Association of Securities Dealers releases short interest figures for its securities. Quite simply, short interest is the number of shares that have been sold short and not yet repurchased. Many analysts look at this indicator as a ratio of short interest to the average daily volume. The so-called "short interest ratio" tells investors how many days worth of trading must take place to completely eliminate the shorts. The higher the number, the greater the bearishness. Because every share sold short must be repurchased at some point in time, large short volumes represent captive demand for the underlying security.

At ISI, we spend a lot of time looking at the short interest ratio for the market in aggregate. Like our survey of hedge funds, persistently high short interest as a percentage of New York Stock Exchange shares outstanding indicated that sentiment was still bearish throughout 2003, providing an important signal to go long heading into 2004 (see Chart 7-3). It is important to remember, however, that companies that have recently issued convertible bonds or are involved in an acquisition may have misleadingly high short interest ratios.

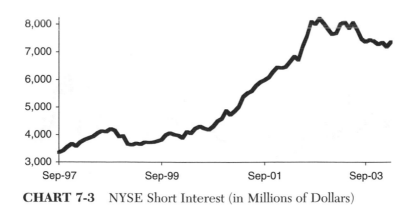

CHART 7-3   NYSE Short Interest (in Millions of Dollars)

The CBOE Volatility Index

This index measures market expectations of near term volatility conveyed by stock index option prices. The CBOE's Web site states that "since volatility often signals financial turmoil, [the] VIX is often referred to as the 'investor fear gauge.'"

Despite some recent changes in its calculation, the VIX provides a window into stock market volatility over the next 30 calendar days. Using a weighted average of options with a constant maturity of 30 days to expiration, the index often registers its highest readings during times of intense financial turmoil and fear, signaling potential opportunities for bargain hunters.

As Chart 7-4 indicates, the VIX reached its highest levels during the Long Term Capital Management and Russian Debt Crises in 1998 and after September 11, 2001. Securing its reputation as an important contrarian indicator, the VIX has also historically tended to move in an opposite direction to its underlying index. Earlier in 2004, relatively low index levels had many investors wondering whether sentiment levels on stocks were too ebullient. But while there was little question that the index was trading at low levels compared with its historic average, a longer-term look at the chart indicates that levels in the mid-teens are far from euphoric. The VIX traded at levels between 10 and 20 from 1991 through1996.

The Put/Call Ratio

Investors also like to look at the ratio of put option volumes (bearish bets) to call option volumes (bullish bets) as some indication of investors' depth of conviction about the market's future direction. The

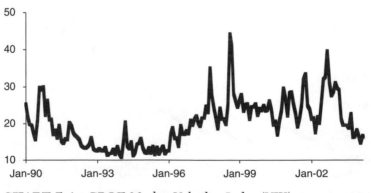

CHART 7-4   CBOE Market Volatility Index (VIX)

CBOE tracks the total volume of options on all equities as well as the volume of S&P 100 Index options. According to *Barron's,* readings of the CBOE equity-put-call ratio of 60:100 and of the S&P 100 of 125:100 are considered bullish, while an equity ratio of 30:100 and an index ratio of 75:100 are considered bearish.

New Issue Activity and Mutual Fund Purchases

New issue activity and mutual fund purchases have also been useful indicators of investor euphoria and apathy. Useful contrarian indicators at extremes indicate the public's willingness to purchase stocks. Early in 2000 one of my clients claimed that the new issue market was so hot that investment banks could probably capitalize a ham sandwich. Hot new issue markets usually accompany more speculative environments and have often preceded market tops. Moribund new issue markets, on the other hand, especially when they occur in tandem with low relative valuations, usually signal greater potential returns.

Investor's Business Daily compares the number of new issues to the total number of stocks on the New York Stock Exchange. The ratio is a quick and efficient way to size up new issue activity. It reached its all-time high of 49.5 percent in March 1987, seven months before the crash. The ratio's low was registered on July 28, 2003, four months after the start of the current bull market.

The public's interest in purchasing equity mutual funds, especially relative to bond funds, can also often signal important potential changes in trend. While strong and steady interest in equity funds provides mutual fund companies with the fuel necessary to propel the market higher, excessive interest can be a hallmark of public greed, which is often associated with market tops. Significant redemptions of equity funds, on the other hand, can signal fear and the selling climax that usually precedes broader advances in the market. As Chart 7-5 shows, the public had enormous interest in equity funds versus bond funds in the first quarter of 2000 just as stocks were peaking. Massive redemptions of equity funds and heavy purchases of bond funds were seen near the lows in stock prices in the summer of 2002, three months before the bottom.

Media Enthusiasm

In addition to the various indicators listed above, investors would be well served to pay attention to the sentiments of the news media. Because markets discount new information far more quickly than

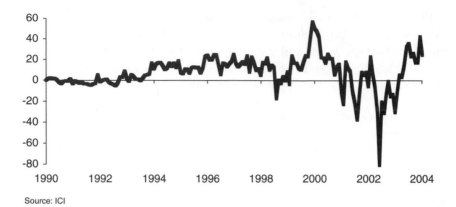

Source: ICI

CHART 7-5 Net Equity Fund Flows Minus Net Bond Fund Flows (in $U.S. Billions)

news sources, excessive negative or positive press coverage often sig-nals an impending change of trend. Interestingly, this "indicator" works just as well at market tops as it does at market bottoms.

BusinessWeek's famous 'The Death of Equities" cover story in 1979, for instance, is often cited as one of the great buying opportunities for stocks of all time, while appearances of CNBC anchors on *The Tonight Show* in the late 1990s should have been, in retrospect, a warning signal to anyone interested in capital preservation. More than a few of my bud-dies have suggested that my appearances on TV were a strong sell-signal.

In July 2002, at the depths of the postbubble market and in the midst of the crisis of confidence caused by corporate scandal, the cov-ers of *BusinessWeek*, *The Economist*, and *Time* took on an extremely cautious tone in the same two week period. Again, the timing of these articles in prominent news magazines suggested that few people did-n't already know how bad the stock market was performing and that the waves of selling were near an end. Although the market would make new lows in October 2002 and test them in March 2003, the S&P was up nearly 30 percent in the next year.

The Importance of Confirmation

While it's always nice to see contrarian indicators flashing risk or opportunity before one puts on a new trade, it's even nicer to have a little confirmation once the trade is made. The best way to do this in the aggregate is to look at the performance of other related markets, like bonds and commodities.

There was little doubt in the beginning of 2003, for example, that a good part of the rally had been fueled by short covering: Short interest as a percentage of NYSE shares outstanding was near a record high, traditional sentiment indicators like Market Vane and the put/call ratio were near oversold levels, and ISI's own proprietary hedge fund survey suggested that speculative money had been largely and enthusiastically short. But in contrast to the July and October lows in 2002, when bond yields continued to fall despite the strength in stocks, the bond yields backed up significantly once the stock rally started in earnest in March 2003, providing an important confirmation that stocks were rising not only because of short covering, but also because of the underlying strength in the economy.

Case Study: The "Coconut Crowd"

A big fan of alliteration, and always amazed at Wall Street's ability to coin new phrases, I got a big kick out of a then new term going around trading desks in early 2003—the "coconut crowd." The phrase was used, in a somewhat pejorative way, to describe investors who expected the market to rally after the war with Iraq started and asked the question, "How can the market rally if everyone holds that view?" While we didn't deny that the majority of investors expected stocks to rally after the United States invaded Iraq, we thought it was clear that few investors had positioned themselves to take advantage of that view. With the market revisiting its October 2002 lows on the cusp of war, it was clear that market sentiment was far from ebullient. This was in contrast to what we experienced in the weeks leading up to the first Gulf war, when both sentiment and market action were arguably more bullish.

Confounding any attempt to determine just how investors feel about stocks is the changing nature of those investing in the market. As we discussed earlier in the chapter, bears often pointed to the exceedingly bullish levels of sentiment indicators, such as Market Vane, Investors Intelligence, and *Barron's* Big Money Poll, as proof that there were few willing buyers of stocks left to propel a significant rally early in 2003.

It was a tough decision, but at ISI we decided to disregard the bearish signals we were receiving from these indicators at the time, believing that they didn't fully capture the feelings of the hedge fund community. This was because we felt that these traditional sentiment indicators came up short in determining the consensus of the market's biggest customers. As we discussed in Chapter 2, anecdotal evidence suggested at the time that hedge funds represented about 35 to 40 percent of the trading volume on the Street and, by extension, at least that amount of the market's daily trading volume.[14] Making matters worse, most professional investors (especially those within hedge funds themselves) viewed the hedge fund industry as a small and elite niche of investors who had no impact on the general sentiment level of the market. This was a major miscalculation. Hedge funds were where the action was, and they were largely short at the time. In essence, hedge funds had become the market and few people had realized it.

Ultimately, we believed a favorable outcome in Iraq would set the stage for a significant rally in stocks for three reasons: (1) The price of oil was likely to decline, (2) the chances of the President getting his tax package through Congress were sure to increase, and (3) short interest was still high.

As it turned out, we were right on two of these three conditions for a market rally. Perhaps the most important was the excessive level of bearishness. While many institutional investors expressed confidence about the outcome of our impending war early in 2003, it was interesting to note that sentiment was far more gloomy on stocks than it had been in the weeks leading up to the first Gulf war.

It's Better to Be Right than "Smart"

In the early days of March 2003, with the market about to retest the October 2002 lows and market bulls on the run, I gave a presentation to a large and storied investment management company that had just started to hire people from outside the firm to run a group of hedge funds in-house. Needless to say, making presentations when you're wrong—or as we often like to say, "early,"—is never fun, but this meeting took on a hostile tone that I had rarely seen before or have seen since.

Despite the market's weakness at the time, we were bullish, believing that earnings would surprise people on the upside and, perhaps more important, that the underlying sentiment on stocks was discounting the worst-case scenario for the economy and America's involvement in Iraq. I remember pointing out the extreme levels of bearishness in our survey of hedge funds to my hosts, 20 rather stern looking men and women, sitting around a large oak conference table.

I said, "Our survey shows there are a lot of people on the short side already. We think that if you're short, you may want to be careful. And if you're long—"

A young man, probably in his 30s, who sat at the end of the table, cut me off. He'd come to the meeting later and now wanted to assert some control over its content. He was one of the new hedge fund managers and was obviously short. "Let me ask you a question," he said. "Where are all the smart people in this business?"

I was dumbfounded. At ISI we have an unwritten rule that describing yourself as "smart" or substituting your own judgment for the market's was the next best thing to a necktie party. Before I could construct some meager response, he answered for me.

"They're at hedge funds, my friend. So I think your firm's little index is going to be a good leading indicator rather than a good contrarian one. Stocks are going down."

The response around the table was a stunned silence punctuated only by furtive glances at me to see if I had already started to gather my things. In not so many words, he was saying, "I'm smart and you're stupid." If I had answered, "Well, all the smart people are right here sitting around this table," I might have been able to cut the tension and move on with my presentation. But such witty comebacks are only witnessed in motion pictures, I'm afraid, and are seldom offered, at least by me, in the course of everyday life.

Instead, I limped home to finish my prepared remarks and left. Of course, I wasn't quite sure my new friend wasn't entirely correct in his assessment of his own intelligence. On the car ride back to my office, questions raced through my brain: Who was I, really, to offer advice to anyone? Was the market down for the count? Were we on the verge of a deflation last seen in the '30s? Who invented liquid soap and why?

As it stood, the market would start a major rally a little more than a week later that would result in a nearly 29 percent total return for the S&P and a 50 percent return for the Nasdaq for the year. This episode taught me two major lessons I will never forget as an investor:

1. Fade stridently held views on the market every time.
2. There's really no such thing as being "smart" in the investment business.

One of the central ironies about the investment business, and perhaps life, is that often the trades one feels most confident about are the ones that result in the biggest losses. The old stock market adage that "the market likes to climb a wall of worry" captures the feeling of most seasoned investment pros that there is very little easy money to be made in stocks. Some of the best opportunities to invest in stocks (August 1982 and October 2002) came at a time when the underlying sentiment about the economy and the stock market couldn't have been much bleaker. It goes without saying that the skeptics and the Cassandras didn't retreat quietly when things started to turn up. To this day, some in the media, and on the presidential trail, carp about our present "jobless recovery." This should be amusing to anyone who has attempted to get a parking space at a shopping mall in the last year. And yet, as we have seen, the media tends to make stars of bearish gurus just when stocks are about to go up, and of bullish seers just as stocks are about to fall.

In retrospect, one of the most interesting things about the story recounted above was how emphatic the antagonist in our story was about his own view. This is a recipe for disaster in the investment world, for there are too many facts to know, and, I don't care who you may be, there's always someone just a little smarter than you. The best and brightest in the investment world have a view, even a strongly held one, but are *always* open to new information and insist on being intellectually flexible.

Ed Hyman was once quoted as attributing his success as an economic forecaster to the fact that he was "almost always uncertain." And Jim Moltz recounted a story about his days as chairman and chief investment strategist of C.J. Lawrence that also underscores how important it is to be intellectually flexible.

On one of his many trips to Boston in the early 1980s, Jim was accosted while crossing the street by an angry client furious that one of C.J.'s analysts had turned to negative on energy stocks. Quite literally grabbing him by the lapels, this client laced into Jim and told him that he was on the verge of ruining his franchise as one of the Street's preeminent providers of independent research. Jim was kind enough to share this story with me in the early days of March 2003, saying, "When people get that strident about their point of view, they are almost always wrong." It almost goes without saying that oil stocks had, at that time, begun their long fall from the grace and glory they had achieved in the late 1970s.

Will Rogers once said, "An economist's opinion is worth as much as anyone else's," and he was right. Given the fact that in the course of my entire education and career I have only worked—or wanted to work, for that matter—in the securities industry, I may be speaking out of school when I say that I can think of no other industry that has as many intellectual pretensions as my own. For whatever reason, people are obsessed with being "smart" on Wall Street. This is pretty silly, really, because, let's face it, analysts and portfolio managers aren't exactly splitting atoms or performing complicated spinal cord surgeries in the course of their working days. And yet, the charade that what finance professionals do for a living requires extraordinary intellectual capabilities continues.

This misplaced self-confidence has grown substantially with the growth of hedge funds and alternative investment vehicles and their outsized returns during the bear market. Perhaps it's necessary to justify a 20 percent cut of the profits, but there are more than a few young analysts at hedge funds whom I've met who insist that they were actually correct, and the market wrong, when they lost money in their positions in 2003. It's as if they believe their clients award them style points if the thought process behind a losing position was sufficiently sophisticated, nuanced, and abstruse.

Several years ago I read a study about Harvard Business School that found that its newly minted MBAs would rarely chart their own career choices and, generally speaking, followed the herd into industries that were just about to peak. In 1987, Harvard grads desperately wanted to enter the merger and acquisition boom on Wall Street. Then came October 1987. In 1989 it was real estate. Oops. In 1999 it was Internet start-ups. Double oops. [15]

This study is important because it suggests that "smart" and educated people are just as likely to succumb to the vicissitudes and whims of crowd behavior as other mere mortals. It obviously rings true to anyone who worked on Wall Street or in Silicon Valley in the late 1990s. This sentiment was captured perfectly in what many consider the seminal work on the subject of crowd behavior, Gustave LeBon's *The Crowd: A Study of the Popular Mind*:

> **In the case of everything that belongs to the realm of sentiment—religion, politics, morality, the affections and antipathies, etc.—the eminent men seldom surpass the standard of the most ordinary individuals. From the intellectual point of view an abyss may exist between a great mathematician and his boot-maker, but from the point of view of character, the difference is often slight or nonexistent.[16]**

Hearing a sell-side analyst or portfolio manager say "I'm right and the market is wrong" should set off alarm bells to any potential client.

There is no antidote to blindly following the consensus except a curious mixture of humility and self-confidence, which has been the consistent and reliable hallmark of great investors like Julian Robertson, George Soros, Peter Lynch, and Warren Buffett. Ultimately, no one in the investment business really cares how smart you are. Performance and performance alone equals smarts in our business. The market is always right. Period.

Key Take-Aways

1. The difference between exceptional investors and those posting lackluster performance often lies in their ability to go against the crowd.
2. Remember: When everyone is bullish, there are only potential sellers; when everyone is bearish, there are only potential buyers.
3. Purchasing shares in any company is a bet not on the present, but on the future.
4. Pick a relatively short list of sentiment indicators to follow and develop a feel for their strengths and shortcomings.
5. Opinion-based indicators are better at forecasting market bottoms than they are at forecasting market tops.
6. Excessive media coverage of a company or industry, either positive or negative, often precedes a major change in trend.
7. The most stridently held views in the investment business are often the most wrong.
8. There are no style points in the investment business. Outperformance is the only true indicator of intelligence.

8

THE IMPORTANCE OF
VALUATION

IT'S ALL ABOUT POTENTIAL

"To know values is to know the meaning of the market."
—CHARLES DOW

ONE OF THE GREATEST DIFFICULTIES for both individual and professional investors alike is to keep in mind that some of the best companies can sometimes be the worst investments. The difference between the prospects for a company and the prospects for its stock often part ways due to valuation. Unfortunately, many market participants employ the "greater fool" theory of investing, whereby little attention is paid to an asset's intrinsic value as long as there exists someone else, similarly unconcerned about valuation, ready to buy.

Although it may appear that successful professional investors are gifted at playing hunches or are merely lucky, successful pros spend a considerable amount of their time and money trying to figure out just what a company is worth, realizing that without some stringent regard for value, it's just a matter of time before they themselves will be the greater fool. The performance of legendary investors like Warren Buffett, Peter Lynch, and John Neff is not due to luck. It was not based on hunches. In almost all cases the successful investor understands better than most that the odds are in your favor when you don't overpay. Valuation disciplines may at times limit returns, but they also can limit risk.

To some, there may be a certain irony in the fact that professional investors spend as much time as they do to determine the underlying value of their investments. Shouldn't large investors with their vastly superior access to information and liquidity be able to outperform without worrying so much about valuation? These days, there are certainly no shortage of hedge funds and other professional speculators that have proven to be gifted at generating returns without much regard to price. But even these talented players would acknowledge that the best way to consistently "beat the Street" over the long term is to look for those nickels trading for four cents—*especially for the individual investor.*

Unfortunately, many individual investors, without the training, time, or confidence of professional investors, spend far less time than they should determining the value of the stocks they buy. This is a shame because any experienced professional investor will tell you that successfully valuing any asset—stocks, bonds, real estate, etc.—will always be more a function of hard work than of intelligence. Peter Lynch, the legendary former portfolio manager of Fidelity's Magellan Fund, one of the most successful mutual funds of all time, was fond of saying that if the individual investor would spend as much time researching a company he was about to buy as he would the purchase of a refrigerator, he would save himself unnecessary heartache and grief. How true.

It's Not Rocket Science

Perhaps remembering the complex formulas from their college finance classes, or intimidated by weighty tomes on valuation in the bookstore, many individual investors become less confident about their ability to value the companies they buy than they should, and instead rely on tips from friends and brokers as the basis for their investment decisions.

You'll never find me claiming that valuing a company is easy. Countless books and academic articles have been written on the subject. Some of the formulas developed could terrify even the most gifted mathematicians. While these abstruse scribbles may be splayed out on office desks and coffee tables to impress and intimidate the uninitiated, they belie a couple of dirty little secrets about the investment business. The first is that valuation will always be as much of an art as it is a science. While the models often employed in valuation analysis may seem coldly clinical, it is the decisions about the inputs into these models that provide the basis for outperformance. Says Aswath Damadoran in his seminal work, *Investment Valuation*, "Valuation is neither the science some of its proponents make it out to be nor the objective search for true value that idealists would like it to become."[1] The second secret about these weighty academic tomes is that no one—and I mean no one—actually reads them.

The typical honest and successful investor will tell you that he rarely relies on anything he learned in business school and that he never uses calculus when making a decision to buy or sell a stock. He relies instead on fifth grade math, basic and realistic assumptions about earnings and interest rates, a lot of hard work, and experience. There are no magic bullets in the pages that follow, just an attempt to provide a basic understanding of the building blocks of valuation and a few simple and straightforward metrics for determining the value of a company in particular and the market in general.

In the simplest terms, there are two ways to determine the value of any asset:

- The *intrinsic value* approach involves determining the future value of the cashflows the asset throws off and then discounting them back by an appropriate interest rate.
- The *comparables* approach involves looking at comparable assets to see how the market values them..

Both approaches have their merits, and most professional investors use some combination of the two in their investment analysis.

Intrinsic Value: Earnings, Inflation, and Interest Rates

Believe it or not, there are only two things the investment analyst must know to determine the precise intrinsic value of any company—the future value of its cashflows (earnings) and the appropriate long-term interest rate to discount those cashflows. This is easier said than done, but again, many new investors are surprised to discover just how simple the math is in determining what value really is.

As Peter Lynch put it in his wildly popular book, *One Up on Wall Street*:

What you're asking here is what makes a company valuable, and why it will be more valuable tomorrow than it is today. There

are many theories, but to me, it always comes down to earnings and assets. Especially earnings. Sometimes it takes years for the stock price to catch up to a company's value, and the down periods last so long that investors begin to doubt that will ever happen. But value always wins out—or at least in enough cases that it's worthwhile to believe it.[2]

After determining what the likely future value of a stock's cashflows will be, the investor then must determine an appropriate interest rate with which to discount these cashflows. This is tricky because the "present value of money" enters the calculation. Since inflation erodes purchasing power over time, a dollar today is worth more than a dollar tomorrow, and so assumptions about inflation and interest rates are crucial in the valuation process.

Because high levels of inflation and interest rates diminish the present value of future cashflows and, consequently, intrinsic value, an investor's willingness to pay for earnings declines as inflation increases. Interest rates have a big impact on what investors are willing to pay for earnings. They're willing to pay higher prices for the growth and yield that stocks can provide when interest rates are low, and are unwilling to pay up when interest rates are high. Higher interest rates often slow down the economy and limit the potential for earnings gains. The lower interest rates are, the greater the value of a firm's future cashflows, and hence the higher the multiple investors will be willing to pay for its earnings.

Although it may be hard to believe today, P/E multiples for the S&P Industrials fell to 6 at the depths of the bear market in 1982, when long-term interest rates approached 15 percent. While there have been many instances in which investors have bid up the prices of stocks despite higher interest rates, history has shown that to be a sucker bet. Considerable evidence of this phenomenon can be seen in the year-over-year change in the S&P and the year-over-year change in 10-year U.S. Treasury yields, which has often provided important warning signals in overextended markets. In September 1987, 10-year Treasury yields were up 29 percent year-over-year at the same time the S&P was up 39 percent. In December 1999, 10-year yields were up 39 percent while the S&P was up 19 percent (see Chart 8-1).

The market may not be cheap today by historical standards, but when one looks at both the relatively low levels of interest rates and of tax rates on equity investments, stocks don't look so expensive. For all

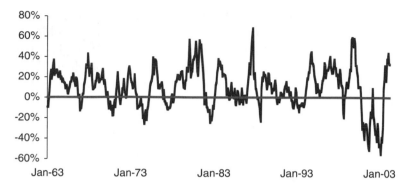

CHART 8-1 S&P 500 Year-to-Year Percentage Change plus 10-Year U.S. Treasury Yield Year-to-Year Percentage Change

the talk of the market going up "too far, too fast," this simple analysis suggests that it has further to run.

P/E Ratio: Linchpin of the Comparable Approach

There is no measure of value more ubiquitous than the price/earnings or P/E ratio, which, simply, is the price of a stock divided by its earnings per share. The beauty of the P/E ratio is its simplicity. No Wharton or Harvard MBA degrees are necessary to figure out this most basic measure of relative valuation. It is important to remember, however, that P/Es don't exist in a vacuum and that they have little value in and of themselves. Their worth is derived from the fact it allows investors to easily determine how expensive a stock is relative to its history and to its peers.

That doesn't mean investors should always buy stocks with low P/Es and sell stocks with high P/Es. Often, a company might sport an out-of-the-ordinary earnings multiple for a good reason. The P/E for a company might be high because of a superior market position or a patent that limits the volatility of its earnings. A stock with a low P/E might be embroiled in legal actions or may be engaged in an industry in secular decline. Still, the P/E ratio does give investors some indication of when the odds are in their favor. To once again quote Peter Lynch, "With few exceptions, an extremely high P/E ratio is a handicap to a stock, in the same way that extra weight in the saddle is a handicap to a racehorse."[3]

A further step in determining value using the P/E ratio is to employ the so-called P/E-to-growth, or PEG, ratio. Based on the old market adage that a stock should never be trading at a multiple higher than its earnings growth rate, the PEG ratio is simply the P/E divided by the expected growth in earnings. Stocks with PEG ratios greater than 1 (the P/E is greater than the expectation of future growth in earnings) are intrinsically more risky than those with PEG ratios below 1.

Which Earnings?

One of the central difficulties in investing in general and valuation in particular these days may be that we have too much information. Nowhere is this more true than when it comes to earnings. Although the P/E ratio is a fairly simple method of applying some consistency to valuing stocks against their peers in the same industry and provides investors with some historical context with which to evaluate both the appeal of stocks and the market as a whole, investors are still left with perhaps one of the most important questions of all—which earnings should they use, forward or trailing, reported or operating, or net income, or earnings per share.

The recent large differences between these various measures have created a situation almost akin to the Tower of Babel in many an investment meeting among institutional investors. Value guys use reported earnings, growth guys use forward measures, and bond guys, well, they use whatever looks most gloomy. Although the choice of which earnings measure to use can be daunting to even the most experienced investor, each metric has its time and place.

Operating vs. Reported Earnings
Separating fact from wishful thinking is often a source of confusion when it comes to quarterly earnings reports. "Reported profits," although rarely used in the media or mentioned at great length in sell-side analyst reports, are based on Generally Accepted Accounting Principles (GAAP) as developed by the Financial Accounting Standards Board (FASB). "Operating" or "pro forma" earnings, on the other hand, are supposed to represent the ongoing revenues and expenses of a firm and often exclude items deemed to be nonrecurring or "extraordinary." Although one would expect some difference between the two figures at any given time, the spread between operating and reported profits widened substantially in the aftermath of the late 1990s bubble. This called into question just how recurring many of these nonrecurring items actually were.

It is important to note that the FASB does allow companies to exclude certain items that reasonable people might consider to be nonrecurring; typically, restructuring charges, the depreciation of goodwill, investment gains and losses, and inventory write-downs. But in the late 1990s companies used extraordinary—some might say ridiculous—methods in their calculation of operating earnings. The *Wall Street Journal* highlighted one transportation company, for example, that excluded the cost of painting its airplanes, clearly a regular business expense, when issuing its quarterly earnings report.

Because companies naturally have a vested interest in deeming every decline in revenues or increase in expenses as "extraordinary" and nonrecurring, this has been, as one might imagine, a constant source of controversy throughout the years. To be fair, in a free market system there is nothing wrong with companies attempting to put their earnings in the best possible light. Companies should be free to issue their own opinions about which expenses are recurring and nonrecurring. The problem comes when companies fail to adequately highlight the differences between their interpretation of earnings and the interpretation required under GAAP. In the bubble years, competition for capital became so intense that even companies wishing to play within the lines were forced to get more aggressive in their accounting just to compete.

This may sound dry to some, but determining the true ongoing earnings potential of a firm is critical to the process of valuation, especially given today's relatively high earnings multiples. For a company trading at 15 times earnings, a recurring expense would have 15 times the impact of a nonrecurring item in the valuation of the firm. As we discussed in Chapter 4, the practice of serial write-offs became widespread in the mid-1990s, when Wall Street largely ignored, at the start of the bull market, the wave of restructuring charges resulting from the 1990–1991 recession.[4]

The difference between operating and reported profits reached its widest point in the fourth quarter of 1999, when Time Warner's $50 billion write-off of its AOL acquisition caused aggregate reported earnings for the S&P 500 to be roughly one-third of operating earnings. Such wide differences clearly make the process of valuation far more difficult for the average investor. The good news, however, is that the combination of new laws, like Sarbanes-Oxley and Regulation G, and serious prosecution of accounting irregularities, have substantially narrowed the differences between these two measures.

Trailing vs. Forward Earnings

There is perhaps no greater source of argument between the "bond guys," as they are affectionately known in our shop, and those of us in equities, than the use of trailing or forward earnings measures. Using trailing earnings rather than forward earnings expectations is a far more conservative way to value companies. The problem is, trailing earnings can be extremely misleading near turning points in the economy—especially near the tail end of recessions when earnings are near their lows.

At the start of 2003 the S&P appeared perilously expensive based on trailing earnings—nearly 28 times trailing reported earnings! That was virtually no different from the height of the bull market peak in 2000. Reflecting a weak economy and massive write-offs, trailing earnings were significantly underestimating the earnings power of the S&P. As it turned out, earnings were up over 18 percent in 2003, making the P/E of the market, in the final analysis, a far more reasonable 22 times trailing, and 18 times forward, at the start of 2004. Because stocks are a discounting mechanism, it makes far more sense to use future earnings expectations in the middle part of the business cycle.

Whither EPS?

The now fairly commonplace practice of "gaming" earnings announcements has forced investors to make another new choice when determining which earnings measure to use: Is the standard practice of issuing earnings-per-share (EPS) the best reflection of a firm's growth in profits?

At first glance many would suspect that there would be no difference between EPS and net income, since EPS is merely net income divided by the total number of shares outstanding. But as we discussed in the chapter on corporate responsibility, the pressure to "make the numbers" has become so intense that many companies have started to use some sophisticated and not so sophisticated methods to make earnings look as impressive as possible. EPS has the benefit of being simple and easy to understand. Unfortunately, it is also subject to manipulation.

By simply buying shares on the open market, companies can decrease the number of shares outstanding and thus boost EPS without any real change in earnings. In the late 1990s, companies routinely bought back shares and engaged in other fancy accounting legerdemain that ultimately weakened the company's balance sheet in an effort to make earnings look more attractive to Wall Street. There is nothing illegal about this, but it does suggest that shareholders should be wary of the impact such practices can have on earnings per share.

Key Top-Down Metrics

Among the institutional investment community, Wall Street often appears to want to put people into categories—small cap versus large cap, value versus growth, and so on. Recent economic difficulties have also revived another important distinction—top-down versus bottom-up. Top-down investors, like strategists, start their investment decisions with a fundamental assessment of the economy's strength and the health of the market in both fundamental and technical terms. They then look for companies in those sectors and industry groups they feel are most likely to benefit (or if they're short-sellers, most likely to get hurt) from the current economic and market environment.

Looking at the market as a whole obviously requires a top-down approach. Determining the relative attractiveness of a broad market measure such as the S&P 500 can often give investors a good idea of whether they should be aggressive in their stock purchases or more defensive. Bottom-up investors, on the other hand, don't concern themselves with the economy at all and concentrate their efforts on finding big differences between a company's intrinsic value and its market value. Most professional investors use a combination of both methods to make their investment decisions. For the purposes of valuing the market as a whole, however, top-down metrics are simpler and easier to understand.

The Fed Model

One of the best top-down measures of stock market valuation is the so-called Fed Model. First mentioned in a relatively obscure Federal Reserve publication, and popularized by Prudential Securities Chief Investment Strategist Edward Yardeni, the model has become the basis upon which top-down players in the financial markets judge the intrinsic value of stocks in aggregate.

Although it sounds somewhat abstruse to the uninitiated, the Fed Model is, in reality, one of the quickest and easiest ways to come to some sort of conclusion about the market's valuation. The model compares the yield on the current 10-year U.S. Treasury to the "earnings yield" of a broad index of stocks (most often the S&P 500). The earnings yield is simply the inverse of the P/E ratio. For example, if a stock is trading at a P/E of 20, it has an earnings yield of 1/20, or 5 percent.

The theory behind the model is also quite simple: At any given time, investors are choosing between only two asset classes—stocks and bonds. Although the Fed Model has had an impressive record of explaining the shift in relative valuations between bonds and stocks (it showed, for instance, that stocks were most overvalued in August 1987, just before the October crash), it is not without its critics. Many have argued that the model leads investors to unrealistic conclusions about what multiple they should pay for earnings at extremely low levels of interest rates. In Japan, as an example, where a decade-long recession pushed long-term interest rates down to 1 percent, the Fed Model would have suggested that stocks should be trading at 100 times earnings. While the model is, admittedly, an oversimplification of the complex task of valuation, it is also an easy way for both individual and institutional investors to determine when the odds are stacked against them or are in their favor.

The Fed Model has widespread appeal among most individual investors not only because of its simplicity and elegance, but also because it has worked. At ISI we made one small adjustment to its most basic calculation that made it even easier for us to determine the relative attractiveness of stocks versus bonds. Instead of converting the S&P 500's P/E multiple into an earnings yield, we put the current long-term bond yield into earnings multiple terms. That is to say, when we see a bond yielding 4 percent, we look at it as trading at 25 times earnings; one yielding 5 percent is trading at 20 times earnings; and so on. This adjustment often feels more comfortable to those accustomed to dealing with equities rather than fixed income investments.

Chart 8-2 shows the Fed Model in P/E terms from May 1995 through March of this year. It is illuminating for anyone who had a front-row seat to the late 1990s bubble years. On December 31, 1999, the Fed Model indicated that the S&P 500 was trading at 27 times forward earnings at the same time bonds were trading at 15 times, a sign that stocks were extremely overpriced relative to bonds. This overvaluation persisted for a while but eventually proved to be unsustainable, as stocks tumbled and bonds rallied over the course of the next three years. Interestingly, the model again proved its worth at the 2003 stock market bottom on March 11. Perhaps more than a coincidence, stocks and bonds made a complete round-trip in multiples. Three years after the historic peak in stock prices, the S&P was trading 15 times earn-

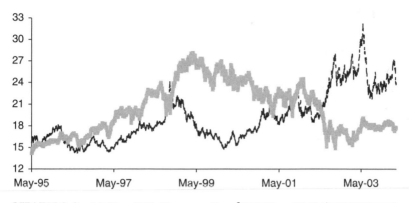

CHART 8-2   10-Year U.S. Treasury Bond "P/E" vs. S&P 500 NTM P/E

ings and bonds were trading at 30 times! Although the model may be flawed, it stands as perhaps the simplest way to get a quick read on the market's relative attractiveness.

Of more interest to many market observers is why the model has worked so well despite the fact that bonds and stocks are such different asset classes. Professor Jeremy Siegel of the Wharton School has suggested it is because the market values the relative advantages of stocks and bonds when inflation is important—bonds provide fixed returns, and stocks are real assets that will vary over time with the general price level—as roughly equal.

The Rule of 20

Another "top-down" method of underscoring the importance of inflation on long-term earnings multiples and offering an assessment of the attractiveness of stocks is the so-called Rule of 20. This method of stock market valuation holds that the addition of the P/E of the market and the inflation rate should equal its long-term average of 20. Readings well above 20 signal stock market overvaluation, while readings well below 20 suggest the presence of cheap stocks. Table 8-1 shows the long-term relationship between stock market P/Es and inflation. It has indeed averaged almost precisely 20 since 1969.

While the Rule of 20 serves the useful purpose of illustrating the impact of inflation on earnings multiples over time, the Fed Model, perhaps because it is based on bond yields and therefore reflects the collective wisdom of the market, does a far better job of offering investors a timely indicator of risk and opportunity in equities in relation to fixed income. This method of stock market valuation was correct in pointing

TABLE 8-1   Rule of 20

Year	Average Price S&P 500	Operating EPS	Average P/E	CPI	Total
1967	89.0	5.33	16.7	3.0	19.7
1968	98.1	5.76	17.0	4.3	21.3
1969	97.7	5.78	16.9	5.5	22.4
1970	81.4	5.13	15.9	5.8	21.7
1971	97.5	5.70	17.1	4.3	21.4
1972	110.4	6.42	17.2	3.3	20.5
1973	106.2	8.16	13.0	6.2	19.2
1974	81.0	8.89	9.1	11.1	20.2
1975	82.8	7.96	10.4	9.1	19.5
1976	99.4	9.91	10.0	5.7	15.7
1977	98.9	10.89	9.1	6.5	15.6
1978	97.0	12.33	7.9	7.6	15.5
1979	103.7	14.86	7.0	11.3	18.3
1980	119.4	14.82	8.1	13.5	21.6
1981	125.5	15.36	8.2	10.3	18.5
1982	122.7	12.64	9.7	6.1	15.8
1983	155.5	14.03	11.1	3.2	14.3
1984	159.1	16.64	9.6	4.3	13.9
1985	187.9	14.61	12.9	3.5	16.4
1986	228.8	14.48	15.8	1.9	17.7
1987	280.4	17.50	16.0	3.7	19.7
1988	263.2	24.12	10.9	4.1	15.0
1989	317.6	24.32	13.1	4.8	17.9
1990	332.2	22.65	14.7	5.4	20.1
1991	364.3	19.30	18.9	4.2	23.1
1992	417.9	20.87	20.0	3.0	23.0
1993	450.0	26.90	16.7	3.0	19.7
1994	459.1	31.75	14.5	2.6	17.1
1995	540.4	37.70	14.3	2.8	17.1
1996	677.8	40.63	16.7	2.9	19.6
1997	860.4	44.01	19.6	2.3	21.9
1998	1085.0	44.27	24.5	1.6	26.1
1999	1326.9	51.68	25.7	2.2	27.9
2000	1427.4	56.13	25.4	3.4	28.8
2001	1194.7	38.85	30.8	2.8	33.6
2002	995.3	46.04	21.6	1.6	23.2
2003	1111.9	54.74	20.4	2.3	22.7
Average			**15.2**	**4.8**	**20.1**

to market overvaluation in the late '90s but was too early in its assessment to be of much use to individual investors seeking to maximize short-to-intermediate term returns or institutional investors wishing to stay employed by coming somewhat close to beating the broader market.

The Importance of Flexibility

Perhaps the most important thing to remember about investing in particular, and valuation in general, is how important it is to remain flexible. Because the market reflects the collective wisdom of all of its participants and is constantly adjusting to changes in fiscal and monetary policies, the geopolitical environment, demographics, etc., sometimes the most tried-and-true valuation yardsticks fail to be as effective as they once were. Until the 1950s, for example, many investors believed that common stocks, because of their inherent risk, should have yields that exceeded those of corporate bonds. In fact in the prior two generations, stocks almost always underperformed, sometimes violently so, anytime dividend yields dipped below those of fixed income securities.

Morgan Stanley's legendary strategist Byron Wien was just starting out on Wall Street in the late 1950s the last time this "evil omen" returned.[5] The older and most senior portfolio managers in his shop, occupying his company's most prized corner offices, all saw this development as a reason to sell stocks. They sold more when dividend yields continued to fall. Unfortunately for them, the market remained in an upward trend. Byron remembers that little by little these men were moved from their corner offices into interior offices until, about 10 years later, they were no longer managing money.

This story provides an object lesson for those relying on, or trying to develop, systems to beat the market: it's perfectly acceptable to use models to value stocks and the market, but they should be altered frequently to account for changes in the economic environment and investor attitudes toward risk.

If I had a dime for every time I saw a new valuation or technical model that would purportedly obviate the need for human beings to make tough decisions about investments, I would grow a beard, have some plastic surgery, and retire to a small island in the Mediterranean. It isn't difficult to come up with systems that work in back-testing. The real difficulty is designing a system that will anticipate the market's attitudes toward risk and return, valuation, and scores of other factors that determine an asset's value. A system that accomplishes these things may exist somewhere, but it seems unlikely that anyone possessing it would be willing to sell it—for any price. For this reason, the important process of valuation will always be a highly sophisticated art form rather than a science. It is also a reason why it pays to be flexible.

Where Are We Now?

First, one could claim that stocks should currently be trading at a bond market multiple of 21 times our 2004 earnings forecast of $66.[6] This would imply a fair value on the S&P of 1,386. Another interpretation, and one we find more prudent, is that the lower earnings multiple on stocks versus bonds suggests that the market is already discounting higher interest rates. In either case, stocks are far cheaper than bonds at current levels, especially when one considers the difference in tax treatment between interest income and capital gains and dividends.

Although it might be hard to claim that the market is cheap today, it seems clear that investors are far more rational in their approach to valuing stocks. Chart 8-3a shows the P/Es of the 50 largest companies in the S&P 500 in the month of the market's peak in March 2000, and Chart 8-3b shows the P/Es of the market's 50 largest companies four years later, in March 2004. Clearly, investors have had a change of heart in what they were willing to pay for future earnings. Multiples compressed dramatically. The difference is even starker when one considers that these P/Es were based on *forward* earnings.

Still, many are quick to point out that even if the P/E on the market as a whole is 18 times, the market is far more expensive than its historical average of 14 to 15 times earnings. This is true, but as we discussed earlier in the chapter, interest rates are near secular lows, and thus justify higher earnings multiples. While rates are now so low that multiple expansion may be difficult to achieve in the coming years (more on this in the next chapter), it can be argued that better central banking and lower tax rates also justify higher-than-average P/Es.

As we discussed in the chapter on dividends, the blended tax rate on equity investments is almost lower than at any time since the tax code was invented in 1913. This is significant given the wealth of empirical evidence that suggests it is after-tax returns that drive investment decisions for both individual and professional investors. So while it may appear that multiples are at nosebleed levels today, a combination of easy monetary and fiscal policies explains why the

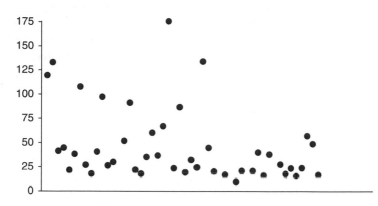

CHART 8-3a   P/Es of the 50 Largest (Market Cap) S&P 500
Companies—March 2000

CHART 8-3b   P/Es of the 50 Largest (Market Cap) S&P 500
Companies—March 2004

market multiple can be higher than what many investors are accustomed to. The Fed Model and the Rule of 20 both suggest that the market is neither too cheap nor too expensive. Of course, these already high P/E levels will make investing more tricky in the coming years and, as we will see in the next chapter, will require skilled active management to achieve double-digit returns.

Key Take-Aways

1. Great companies don't always make good investments. The difference between the two lies in valuation.

2. For the individual investor, the P/E ratio is probably the simplest and most efficient way of judging a firm's value. Its power is derived when one uses it to compare a company to its historical valuation or against companies in the same industry.
3. Big differences between operating and reported earnings should be a considered warning signs for investors. Fortunately, strict accounting legislation is diminishing the differences between these two measures.
4. Using trailing earnings rather than forward earnings expectations is a far more conservative way to value companies. Easier said than done, trailing earnings should not be used at turning points in the business cycle.
5. Top-down metrics of market valuation like the Fed Model and the Rule of 20 suggest that the market is fairly valued.
6. Low interest rates and cuts in tax rates on capital gains and dividends justify higher than average earnings multiples.

9

BRINGING IT ALL TOGETHER

THE MARKET BALANCE SHEET AND THE THRIFTY FIFTY

*"The race may not always go to the swift or the victory
to the strong, but that's the way to bet."*
—Damon Runyon

A FRIEND OF MINE ONCE described the difference between the
buy-side and the sell-side as somewhat akin to the difference between
majoring in chemistry and majoring in psychology—in chemistry you
actually have to come up with the right answer. Given the challenges
inherent in managing money, you wonder why so many sell-siders fan-
tasize about being on the buy-side. Perhaps it's the potential for access
to box seats at Shea. Or perhaps it's merely the allure of being able to
ask questions rather than answer them.

In truth, I too have often wondered what I would ask a sell-side
strategist like myself in order to move past the standard presentation
and get to the bottom line. "What's the weakest part of your thesis?" or
"What would make you change your mind?" aren't bad, but ultimately
I've decided that one simple solitary question would do the trick:
"What's the last trade you made in your personal account?" The honest
answer to that question will tell you more about a strategist's view of
the economy and the stock market than any number of pages of sector
weights, earnings projections, and "thought" pieces.

After eight chapters of holding forth on such issues as dividends,
winner-take-all global markets, and valuation, it's probably time to

open the kimono on the methods I use in determining the answers to two questions:

1. Should I put more money to work in stocks?
2. What types of stocks should outperform in the years to come?

Of course, this is hardly the be-all and end-all of stock investing, but it's only fair if I share with you my own thoughts about the market and the stocks I've been buying in my own portfolio.

There's little question that navigating the U.S. economy and, by extension, stocks, can be fraught with peril. Debt levels remain high, further consolidation is likely and necessary in any number of industries, oil prices are sticky, and geopolitical risks remain. But in my view, after the brutal bear market that started in March 2000, valuations and investor sentiment are sufficiently restrained to pave the way for higher stock prices as the economic recovery matures. What follows is an examination of the methods I use when constructing my own portfolio.

The Market Balance Sheet

As uncertainty surrounding the economy and the market grew after September 11, I resurrected an analytical tool first developed by legendary investor and former Goldman Sachs chief Investment strategist, Lee Cooperman. The Market Balance Sheet exercise is deceptively simple: Determine whether the key drivers of stock prices are headwinds or tailwinds for stocks.

With my mentor, Jim Moltz, and my right-hand man, Nick Bohnsack, I have isolated 15 key drivers of stocks throughout the years. Once a month we look at each of these drivers and force ourselves to classify them as assets or liabilities. Like the balance sheet of any company, the difference between the number of assets and liabilities is our shareholders' equity, and gives us a good idea whether we should be increasing or decreasing our exposure to stocks. In many cases our assessment of these elements is unclear. But we came to the conclusion long ago that getting the "right" answer is less important than the discipline of sitting down once a month and testing the basic tenets upon which we rest our opinions of the market.

One of the chief difficulties for any financial analyst, professional or amateur, is to be intellectually fresh and honest. I have often made the mistake of believing my thinking was up to date on a key driver for stock prices like valuation, only to learn later that I had missed a new and important development. Regularly testing one's investment theses is a crucial element of risk management. As a result, at ISI we have increasingly tried to develop disciplined, though not rigid, exercises to shape our approach to investing.

The 15 key drivers of stock prices can be broadly separated into two categories: fundamental and environmental factors. The fundamental factors driving stock market performance (Table 9-1a) comprise those elements that go to the heart of the performance of the economy as a whole and the relative attractiveness of stocks. The environmental factors (Table 9-1b) deal more broadly with those external forces that might augment or limit an investor's confidence when deciding to put more money to work in common stocks.

While virtually every investor will have his or her own opinion about the drivers of stock prices, it might be worthwhile to offer the process by which we determine whether certain environments favor greater risk or greater caution.

Fundamental Factors

1. Profit Growth/Margins
Perhaps the greatest single driver of stock prices is not necessarily the level of earnings, but the rate of change in earnings estimates and profit margins. For the most part, investors should be putting more money to work in stocks when earnings and profit margins are increasing and taking money off the table when earnings decline. Because Wall Street is typically late in catching changes in trends, monitoring

TABLE 9-1a ISI Market Balance Sheet: Fundamental Factors	**TABLE 9-1b** ISI Market Balance Sheet: Environmental Factors
1. Profit Growth/Margins	1. Administration
2. Economic Growth	2. Free Trade/Protectionism
3. Valuations	3. Monetary Policy
4. Inflation	4. Fiscal Policy
5. Sentiment	5. War vs. Peace
6. Technical Picture	6. Liquidity
7. Demographics	7. Fiscal Health
	8. Value of Dollar

both positive and negative earnings surprises versus expectations is often a good way to determine the path of least resistance for stock prices. According to the popular "cockroach" theory, negative earnings surprises are often a harbinger of a change in trend. Once there's one, more are sure to follow.

Current Assessment: Asset. S&P 500 earnings are poised to be up 20 percent in 2004 due to a strengthening economy, a weaker dollar, and significant operating leverage.

2. Economic Growth

If profits are the underlying theme upon which stock prices move, economic growth provides the rhythm. While determining what part of the economic cycle in which you find yourself has major implications for stock and sector selection, merely knowing whether the economy is growing or contracting is enough to determine whether investors should be increasing or decreasing their exposure to stocks. The initial phase of an economic recovery is the best time to invest in stocks. Investor optimism is often at its lowest, and valuation concerns at their highest. This ensures good entry points for stock investment. Later stages of economic recovery are often the riskiest times to be in stocks, given the Fed's desire to raise rates and soak up liquidity.

Current Assessment: Asset. A combination of fiscal and monetary stimulus, inventory rebuilding, and strong corporate profits bode well for 2004 economic growth.

3. Valuations

There is perhaps no more important exercise for a financial analyst when considering a new investment than determining its intrinsic value. While valuing the market as a whole is in some ways more difficult than valuing individual securities, at ISI we generally rely on two simple valuation metrics to determine whether the market is cheap or expensive: the so-called Rule of 20 and the Fed Model. Historically, add up the P/E of the market to the current inflation rate has equaled 20. Given the strong relationship between the inflation rate and earnings multiples, the Rule of 20 holds that stocks are expensive when the sum is above 20 and cheap when it's below 20. Under the assumptions of the Fed Model, fair value for stocks occurs when the earnings yield on the market (the inverse of the P/E) is equal to the yield on the 10-year Treasury.

Current Assessment: Asset. While the Rule of 20 suggests that the market is fairly valued, the low level of long-term interest rates make the earnings yield of the broader market very attractive relative to bond yields.

4. Inflation

An important derivative of monetary policy is obviously the rate of inflation. There have been considerable contributions from the academic community demonstrating the inverse correlation between the rate of inflation and P/E ratios, and the historical record is clear: Earnings multiples fell to single digits in the midst of the hyperinflation of the '70s and soared to near 30 times as inflation declined in the late 1990s. While it can be argued that stocks become more attractive than bonds as inflation rises because companies themselves can raise prices, persistently high inflation rates have lowered the value of financial assets.

Current Assessment: Asset. The inflation rate is still historically low but is showing signs that it may rise.

5. Sentiment

As we saw in Chapter 7, investors should put more money to work when stock prices reflect widespread pessimism and take money off the table when they reflect widespread optimism. Empirical evidence has suggested that sentiment indicators have been more effective in predicting future movements of security prices at oversold rather than overbought levels. Our collective experience in the late 1990s may be some evidence of this phenomenon: Investor sentiment remained euphoric for several years.

Current Assessment: Asset. While investors are far more sanguine about the prospects for the economy and the market than they were in March 2003, at the market's low, widespread concerns about valuations, the budget deficit, inflation, and geopolitical tensions persist. Investor sentiment is far from euphoric.

6. Technical Picture

While academics have long scoffed at the "science" of observing the price and volume patterns that lie at the center of technical analysis, there isn't a professional investor I know who doesn't spend considerable time looking at charts. Though it may be difficult to discern short-term price movements from the study of charts (or the study of anything, for that matter), being broadly aware of the market's overall trend is crucial in determining the risk profile of a portfolio. At ISI we have found that relying on one simple technical indicator—the 200-day moving average—has saved us a lot of pain. Simply put, we are inclined to take more risk when a stock or an index breaks its 200-day moving average to the upside when the moving average itself is flat or rising, and to be more cautious if prices breach the 200-day average when the average itself is flat or declining (see Chart 9-1).

Current Assessment: Asset. The S&P 500 remains well above its 200-day moving average, indicating that the broader trend for the market is still bullish.

7. Demographics

Theories put forward by Nobel Prize–winning economists Milton Friedman and Franco Modigliani hold that people's spending and savings decisions are generally based on their long-term expectations of income, rather than on receipts during some arbitrary accounting period such as a year. This suggests that population trends can have major implications on investors' willingness to buy stocks and bonds. Essentially, younger people are more willing to buy risky assets like stocks because they believe they can ride out the volatility usually associated with them, while older people tend to sell equities in favor of fixed income securities. Some market forecasters, like Harry Dent, believe that the demographic most favorable to equity investing is the number of people in their late 40s, when the proclivity to spend and to save is at its highest.

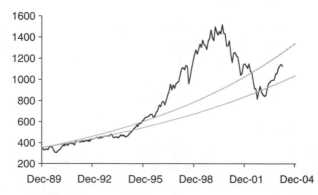

CHART 9-1 S&P 500 vs. Projected 10% and 8% Compound Annual Return

Current Assessment: Asset. The number of 25- to 64-year-olds will continue to grow until 2008-09.

Environmental Factors

8. Administration

As we saw in Chapter 3 with the conflict between President Kennedy and U.S. Steel, whether investors believe an administration is pro- or antibusiness can have an enormous impact of the performance of stocks. Certainly few, if any, Presidents have been outwardly hostile to big business, but an administration's attitudes toward taxes and regulation can set the tone for an investor's willingness to put incremental money to work in stocks. While Kennedy's showdown with U.S. Steel stands as an example of how perceptions of an antibusiness administration can damage investor confidence, President Reagan's controversial decision to fire strikers from the air traffic control union suggested that his administration would be far more probusiness. Reagan's decision, along with his tax cuts, provided fallow ground for the '80s boom in stocks.

Current Assessment: Asset. Investors and businessmen alike have cheered President Bush's three tax cuts (including cuts in capital gains and dividends). The imminent election, however, may change those perceptions.

9. Free Trade/Protectionism

In today's global economy, businesses have become increasingly dependent upon free trade as a means to both buy low-cost inputs and as a source of new markets for finished goods. Trade barriers increase the cost of doing business and can have deleterious effects on inflation, long-term interest rates, and, ultimately, earnings multiples. The stock market has a clear preference for economic environments in which protectionist sentiments are quiescent. Some have seen the present administration's decision to erect trade barriers on steel as one of the contributing factors in the market's sell-off in 2002.

Current Assessment: Liability. Unfortunately, the Bush administration and his chief Democratic rival have determined that protectionism sells.

10. Monetary Policy

Of all of the items on our list of key drivers of stock prices, there is perhaps none more important than the market's confidence in the Federal

Reserve to maintain price stability. Knowing whether the Fed is pursuing an "accomodative" (inclined to lower rates) or a "restrictive" (inclined to raise rates) monetary policy should be a significant factor in determining whether investors put more money to work in stocks. Interest rate policy sets the entire tone for the economy and the relative attractiveness of stocks versus other financial assets. Lower rates make the cost of capital cheaper for businesses to expand, allow banks to ease credit to consumers, and make bonds relatively less attractive to investors. Stocks, in turn, become more attractive to investors wishing to capitalize on the improved prospects for the economy. Of course, the steeper the yield curve,[1] the more expansive banks will be with credit, and the greater the prospects for the economy.

Current Assessment: Asset. Although the Fed is indeed raising rates, it continues to maintain a policy stance that is far from restrictive.

11. Fiscal Policy

Broadly speaking, the more confident investors are in the ability of the federal government to keep a tight lid on its own spending while at the same time offering tax policies that encourage spending and investment, the more confident they will be about the prospects of both the economy and the market. In the 1970s a combination of runaway inflation, confiscatory tax policies, and growth in the size of the federal government gave investors few reasons to buy long-term financial assets like stocks. The current President Bush's decision to lower the tax rates on both capital gains and dividends, in contrast, made the after-tax return on stocks more attractive than it had been in nearly 70 years and helped put an end to the bear market that started in 2000.

Current Assessment: Asset. While the Bush administration's spending policies are worrisome, their willingness to cut personal and business taxes presently provides fertile ground for investing in stocks.

12. War vs. Peace

As we saw in Chapter 3, geopolitical concerns can have a significant impact on the willingness of private and professional investors alike to put money to work in the stock market. Not surprisingly, it appears that the market makes clear and accurate assessments about those conflicts it deems as relatively short-lived and those it believes create systemic risk to the world order. Stocks performed relatively well during the Korean conflict, the first Gulf war, and in World War II once it appeared the tide had turned for the Allies. The market struggled, however, during the long years of the Vietnam War and in the initial stages of the war on terror.

Current Assessment: Liability. While it does appear that some progress is being made in Iraq, the cost of America's involvement in the region, both financially and in human terms, is greater than most had anticipated. The war on terror may be as long and as costly as the Cold War.

13. Liquidity

Monetarists like Milton Friedman have long maintained that "inflation is always and everywhere a monetary phenomenon." This concept can, of course, be applied to rising prices of financial assets as well. Ultimately, it's not enough for the Fed to have an "accommodative" monetary policy—there must be evidence that the Fed is creating money. For example, market pundits and portfolio managers alike waited with eager anticipation for the weekly money supply figures to be released during the inflationary period of the 1970s. While the disintermediation of the banking system has caused many investors to pay far less attention to the weekly figures today, at ISI we spend a lot of time tracking the relative trends in broad money aggregates like M3 plus commercial paper. Simply put, money growth in excess of nominal growth in GDP provides the liquidity necessary for growth in financial assets.

Current Assessment: Asset. A combination of low short-term interest rates and strength in bank lending has M3 plus commercial paper growing at double-digit growth rates, which is far faster than the growth in nominal GDP.

14. Fiscal Health

Significant lags in both fiscal and monetary policy mean that it isn't enough for the administration or the Fed to be pursuing expansionary policies. As discussed at length in the last chapter, burgeoning budget deficits eventually result in higher long-term interest rates and can limit the government's ability to provide stimulus through tax and spending policies when needed. While stocks shrugged off growing budget deficits in the 1980s and last year, a growing sense that these deficits are structural rather than cyclical could have a meaningful impact on the upward trajectory of stocks.

Current Assessment: Liability. While the deficit as a percentage of GDP remains well within the historical range, it is growing quickly and may force whatever administration is in Washington to either cut spending or raise taxes—neither of which is a particularly good development for stock prices.

15. Value of the Dollar

While the Fed has generally regarded the value of the dollar with "benign neglect," believing that dollar strength will be derivative of sound monetary policies, stocks generally perform better when administrations pursue a strong currency. A strong dollar has salutary effects on both inflation and long-term interest rates and thus can have a significant impact on earnings multiples and the willingness of foreign investors to purchase U.S. stocks and bonds. As an example, persistent weakness in the U.S. dollar is often cited, along with a significant backup in bond yields, as one of the major contributing factors in the 1987 crash.

Current Assessment: Liability. The trade-weighted dollar was down nearly 10 percent in 2003. Perhaps more important, the Treasury secretary has appeared content with a weaker dollar, and the administration is pursuing more protectionist trade policies.

The Market Balance Sheet in Practice

The Market Balance Sheet concept can be expanded to keep track of more specific industry groups and securities. Last year at ISI we decided to include balance sheets on each of the S&P's 10 sectors. At the start of this new monthly project, we faced the question of whether we should be forward looking in our analysis about the various building blocks of performance, or use a fairly specific methodology to characterize each element as an asset or a liability at a specific point in time. In an effort to be as objective as possible, we came down on the side of assessing each element at the current time. But because investing will always be an art rather than a science, and the Achilles heel of any balance sheet is that it is merely a snapshot, rather than a leading indicator, the Market Balance Sheet is an input into our market and sector calls but is hardly the final word.

On balance, there are more positive drivers in 2004 for stocks than negative drivers, favoring additional investments in equities. Putting it all together, our Market Balance Sheet at midyear is pictured in Table 9-2.

TABLE 9-2   ISI Market Balance Sheet: January 2004 Ledger

ASSETS	LIABILITIES
Economic Growth	Sentiment
Profit Growth/Margins	Free Trade/Protectionism
Technical Picture	Value of Dollar
Fiscal Policy	Fiscal Health
Demographics	War vs. Peace
Inflation	Liquidity
Monetary Policy	**Shareholders' Equity +3**
Administration	
Valuations	

The fact that there are more assets than liabilities puts the odds of success firmly in favor of additional equity investments. Thus, I personally put more money into stocks in April 2003 and again in the early months of 2004. In the next section, I'll discuss my thought process in choosing certain types of stocks after making the decision to invest more heavily in the stock market. The stocks I chose relied on a screen to weed out the companies I thought had the best chances of success in the decade ahead.

The Thrifty Fifty

The nearly three years between the bull market high in March 2000 and the bear market low in October 2002 was not kind to my personal account or to the accounts of almost everyone else. But with a significant portion of my funds languishing in cash, where money market funds yielded 0.6 percent in April 2003 (before taxes, inflation, and the expense ratio), I took note of the positive signals we started to receive from our Market Balance Sheet. And in the spring of 2003, I began thinking once again about making significant investments in the equity markets.

The practice of sell-side analysts revealing what they do in their own personal accounts is practically unheard of, if only because it leaves them open for criticism from friend and foe alike. But I decided to write about my decision, thinking: How often am I going to get the chance to open myself up to ridicule and lose a ton of money at the same time?

But it's a new era on Wall Street, and while what follows is not a recommendation to buy any of the stocks listed, I hope it can serve as an example of how strategists and other macro types might go about developing a "top-down" portfolio. That is to say, I started with my basic assumptions about the economy, inflation, investor sentiment, and interest rates, and then attempted to select stocks that should benefit from that type of economic environment. This approach is very different from a strict "bottom-up" analysis that, in contrast, focuses only on an individual stock's ability to generate earnings, and largely ignores the underlying trend of the economy.

While the jury is still out on which style is more effective, most professional investors and market pundits use a combination of both methods when making their investment decisions. Trained by one of Wall Street's best economists, Ed Hyman, and hardly being an expert at accounting personally, I have found it far easier to use a top-down approach.

In many respects, the decision to invest in stocks is less difficult than deciding upon the stocks in which you should specifically invest. As we discussed in the first part of this chapter, the Market Balance Sheet firmly favored putting additional funds into stocks. But also as we've discussed in previous chapters, it seemed likely that the stock types that would outperform in the decade ahead would be markedly different that those that outperformed in the two decades just past.

First and foremost, because interest rates were so low, and because President Bush had already taken the unprecedented step of lowering taxes on both dividends and capital gains, it seemed that investors would be unable to rely upon multiple expansion as a contributor to total return. Furthermore, higher interest rates and a more precarious geopolitical backdrop will make it essential for investors to choose stocks that could weather bad times, increase their dividends, and abandon the "valuations don't matter" approach of the late 1990s.

Of course, financial history is replete with examples of times when investors lost their senses and were able to justify paying any price for stocks merely because they were going up. The "Nifty Fifty" stocks of the early 1970s immediately come to mind as most similar to the 1990s and relevant. The forebears of tech stocks a generation later, consumer-oriented companies of that period, like Polaroid, incorporated such optimistic and in many ways outlandish growth assumptions that they were considered to be "one-decision" stocks: that is, investors would only have to make one decision about them in their lifetime—to buy them.

Believing that such arrogance and optimism never works out that well in the long run for investors, I came to the conclusion that the characteristics of the stocks I would choose for my own account, and would thus recommend to our institutional investors, would be diametrically opposed to the one-decision tech stocks of the late 1990s.

I wanted to screen for certain characteristics that would stand the test of time and also provide me with a list of companies that I thought had a reasonable chance of increasing dividend payments and of seeing their multiples expand. Believing wholeheartedly in the winner-take-all global economy as discussed in Chapter 5, I wanted to choose only the best companies that survive under almost any circumstances and in which economies of scale mattered—in essence, a new Nifty Fifty in which a small number of companies will see multiple expansion and price appreciation. But unlike the original "one decision" stocks of a generation ago, this group should attract attention from investors not based on starry-eyed growth assumptions, but on solid fundamental factors: operating leverage, a strong balance sheet, and yield. This 50 won't be nifty, but rather thrifty. The result was a new "Thrifty Fifty Screen" comprised of companies that had the following attributes:

Large, Liquid, and Well-Known
It may take many years before the average investor gets over the stunning losses of both wealth and confidence, experienced when investing in stocks and mutual funds. As a result, confidence in the stock market will grow only slowly and will likely be built not on the speculative companies of the late '90s but on large and solid companies that have a proven record of making it through tough times.

When I first got into the business years ago, the term "blue chip" was widely used to express the notion of conservative equity investments. With more than $2 trillion in money market funds earning less than 1 percent today, investors are likely to move, albeit haltingly, into stocks of companies they know. Foreign investors have been huge net sellers of equities in the last several years as well. It is likely they will also gravitate toward the largest and most liquid names when putting money to work in the United States.

Less Leveraged than Their Competition
While the Fed and the administration are doing their best to boost the economy, it seems unlikely that inflation is ready to take off any time soon and that policymakers would make the same mistakes their predecessors did in the 1970s.

As a hangover of the heady days of the bubble, deleveraging and consolidation will likely be a feature of American finance in the next several years. This will eventually be a problem for heavily leveraged individuals and companies, since it's never so expensive to hold debt as when inflation is low and declining. In this environment, heavily leveraged companies leave themselves wide-open to competition from companies with clean balance sheets that can more easily lower prices and put their competitors out of business.

Dividend Payers

As we discussed in the first chapter, individual and institutional investors both are starting to realize that the absence of dividends removes an essential safety net for investors in common stocks, that all companies are not growth companies, and that while it's relatively easy to play fast and loose with the income statement, it's difficult to fake a dividend check. The hard-fought nature of the debate to lower the taxes on dividends and capital gains made investors realize that nearly 50 percent of their return from large cap stocks came from dividends historically. In this environment, companies that offer a yield should attract the attention of long-term investors.

In an effort to stress these characteristics, I created a screen, with the help of data provider FactSet, that required stocks in the S&P 1500 to:

1. Have market caps greater than $2.5 billion
2. Pay a dividend
3. Have growth in free cashflow per share of greater than 10 percent over the last five years
4. Have an average total debt to total equity ratio of between zero and 50 percent over the last five years

This exercise yielded 50 companies, and thus was born the Thrifty Fifty (Table 9-3).

It is important to note that the Thrifty Fifty is merely a "screen" of companies I believe are likely to outperform in the years to come. It is not a portfolio that has been back-tested or designed to be widely diversified. Of course, I realize that the decision to put more money to work in stocks looks well-timed now, and thus might seem self-serving. But rest assured that there may be any number of times in the next few years in which this decision will look, well, just plain stupid. Still, I hope the Market Balance Sheet and Thrifty Fifty exercises provide a small window into how a strategist might evaluate the market and the types of stocks that might outperform.

TABLE 9-3 ISI Thrifty Fifty*

		2Q 2004 CLOSE	DIVIDEND YIELD	5-YR GROWTH FREE CF	5-YR AVG DEBT-TO-EQUITY
PFE	Pfizer	35.05	1.94	31.6	42.9
JNJ	Johnson & Johnson	50.72	1.89	18.9	19.7
MRK	Merck & Co	44.19	3.35	41.9	47.6
PEP	PepsiCo	53.85	1.19	10.5	33.8
UPS	United Parcel Service	69.84	1.60	39.7	33.9
VIA.B	Viacom	39.21	0.61	40.4	26.1
MMM	3M Co	81.87	1.76	59.1	45.2
MDT	Medtronic	47.75	0.61	49.0	17.3
UNH	UnitedHealth Group	64.44	0.05	32.2	35.5
ALL	Allstate Corp	45.46	2.46	26.0	21.2
CAH	Cardinal Health	68.90	0.17	36.7	36.8
MET	MetLife	35.68	0.64	52.0	38.6
CCU	Clear Channel Communications	42.35	0.94	12.2	44.3
ADP	Automatic Data Processing	42.00	1.33	27.3	2.9
ITW	Illinois Tool Works	79.23	1.21	-4.2	27.7
STM	STMicroelectronics NV	23.60	0.25	58.1	41.4
TOC	Thomson Corp	30.86	2.40	22.7	44.1
PGR	Progressive Corp	87.60	0.11	39.8	33.4

TABLE 9-3 (Continued)

		2Q 2004 CLOSE	DIVIDEND YIELD	5-YR GROWTH FREE CF	5-YR AVG DEBT-TO-EQUITY
HIG	Hartford Financial	63.70	1.76	39.0	32.2
ADI	Analog Devices	48.01	0.17	16.1	29.4
GD	General Dynamics	89.33	1.61	23.6	37.0
SLF	Sun Life Financial Services	26.86	2.36	23.8	11.9
HDI	Harley-Davidson	53.34	0.60	33.9	34.6
MHP	McGraw-Hill Companies	76.14	1.58	40.3	35.3
DHR	Danaher Corp	93.37	0.11	23.8	39.1
CB	Chubb Corp	69.54	2.24	22.9	21.7
JHF	John Hancock Financial	43.69	0.80	13.8	27.0
SPLS	Staples	25.32	0.79	111.3	28.3
PFG	Principal Financial Group	35.63	1.26	14.6	36.2
XL	XL Capital Ltd	76.04	2.54	75.8	20.2
LTD	Limited Brands	20.00	2.40	50.9	20.7
EL	Estee Lauder	44.34	0.68	18.9	24.9
BMET	Biomet	38.36	0.23	21.8	7.3
MBI	MBIA	62.70	1.53	15.8	44.6
WPO	Washington Post	884.41	0.79	12.6	49.8
CI	CIGNA Corp	59.02	2.24	26.0	31.1

ABK	AMBAC Financial Group	73.78	0.60	24.9	18.7
CF	Charter One Financial	35.36	2.94	42.7	24.6
CINF	Cincinnati Financial	43.45	2.53	29.3	10.3
MTG	MGIC Investment	64.23	0.23	13.4	18.3
LM	Legg Mason	92.78	0.65	12.9	48.9
MYL	Mylan Laboratories	22.73	0.53	87.2	2.6
TMK	Torchmark Corp	53.79	0.82	20.5	30.3
MOLX	Molex	30.39	0.33	24.0	1.6
COL	Rockwell Collins Corp	31.61	1.14	107.7	9.2
SHW	Sherwin-Williams Co	38.43	1.77	12.7	41.9
VFC	VF Corp	46.70	2.23	31.1	45.8
SFA	Scientific-Atlanta	32.34	0.12	56.8	0.3
RE	Everest Re Group	85.44	0.43	59.4	26.7
GRMN	Garmin Ltd	42.71	1.17	57.3	7.5

* 2Q 2004 Thrifty Fifty

Key Take-Aways

1. Frequent assessments of the risks and opportunities presented by stocks can be an effective method of determining when to put more money to work in the market.
2. The key drivers of stocks can be separated into two categories: fundamental and environmental factors.
3. The types of companies that will outperform in the current decade will be different than those that outperformed in the 1990s.
4. Companies that have relatively low levels of debt, strong growth in free cashflow, and an appreciation of the importance of dividends will likely be the best place to be.

10

THE CASE FOR ACTIVE MANAGEMENT

THE FUTURE OF MUTUAL FUNDS

"Lack of money is the root of all evil."
—GEORGE BERNARD SHAW

THE HISTORY OF WALL STREET is often marked by small, seemingly unrelated events that come together to produce truly revolutionary changes in the size and structure of the financial markets. Although few recognized its significance at the time, Wells Fargo's decision to start the nation's first index fund in 1971 (in collaboration with future Nobel Prize winners in economics Fischer Black and Myron Scholes) could certainly be seen as the single first act of heresy against the established structure of Wall Street, one that would fan the flames of revolution in the investment community. Funded with $6 million from Samsonite's pension fund, the portfolio consisted of 1,000 equally weighted stocks traded on the New York Stock Exchange.[1]

The creation of the country's first index fund, along with the growing popularity of efficient market theories and the emergence of the S&P 500 Index as the single most important benchmark for stock market returns, gave the concept of passive investing or simply investing in an index of stocks—its competitive start against the more traditional concept of active management, where portfolio managers try to beat the overall market through superior stock selection and sector rotation. The appeal of indexation got a further boost by an important article on the subject entitled "The Loser's Game," in which Greenwich

Capital founder Charles Ellis likened investing to amateur tennis and golf. In these "loser's games" he argued, the dominant role of highly skilled professionals made it difficult to win big, giving its participants a strong incentive to avoid errors rather than swinging for the fences.[2]

Although as Mao once put it, "a single spark can light a prairie fire," index investing didn't take off right away. Ironically, the emergence of index funds for pension plans in the late 1970s got started at the same time that active managers began to beat the S&P 500 handily. Indeed, in 1975, only $100 million, or 0.1 percent, of the market was passively invested. Jack Bogle and the Vanguard Group launched its first S&P 500 Index fund aimed at retail investors in the spring of 1975. While heady days of stock market returns in the 1980s and '90s still prompted most investors to try to shoot the lights out with good active managers, more retail and institutional investors began to see the appeal of the lower costs and tax efficiency of passive investing. By 1991, $235 billion had been passively invested in the S&P 500; by 2000, the figure had swelled to $1.25 trillion.[3]

After three consecutive down years for the broader market from 2000 to 2002, many individual investors, bombarded with tales of gross corporate malfeasance and other, less dramatic wrongdoing on the part of some mutual fund managers, continue to wonder whether they should abandon the hope of active management in favor of indexation. There can be little doubt that the corporate scandals of the last few years have done more to bolster the case for passive investing than Jack Bogle and Vanguard have done since their index fund's inception. The argument that the "system is rigged against the little guy" has become so commonplace these days as to become conventional wisdom. But as with most things in the markets, what often appears most obvious often turns out to be wrong. And while the last several years have proven that equity investing is not for the faint of heart, it is exactly the current level of trepidation that once again heightens the allure of active management.

The case for active over passive management rests on three basic elements:

1. The prospects for more moderate and stable returns in the next few years should benefit the skilled stock picker.
2. Low nominal growth environments create winner-take-all markets.
3. Indexed assets have become so large that they will likely be easy marks for experienced active managers.

We'll go into each of these reasons to stick with active managers.

More Moderate and Stable Returns

If this book had been published in January 1981, the Fed funds rate would be 20 percent, inflation would be running at double-digit rates, and the unemployment rate would be approaching 10 percent. As bleak as the situation seemed, it was one of the great springboards for equity investing of all time. Why?

Not only did investors benefit from the rebound in economic growth and corporate profits brought about by the Reagan administration's stimulative fiscal policies, but they also saw a significant improvement in the market's willingness to pay-up for earnings due to responsible monetary policy. In essence, things couldn't have been much worse to start the decade.

Stocks were cheap. The P/E ratio in the S&P Industrials fell to 6 and the dividend yield was over 5 percent. Only a few astute investors and market commentators began buying stocks at the time, recognizing their potential if the Fed could restore the market's confidence in its ability to rein in inflation. Fortunately, the ineffectual monetary policies of Fed Chairman Arthur Burns gave way to one of the greatest inflation fighters of all time: Chairman Paul Volcker. His Herculean efforts to control inflation set the stage for a massive decline in both long- and short-term interest rates.

Given the strong relationship between inflation and earnings multiples discussed in the last chapter, this dramatic decline in interest rates was an enormous tailwind for higher earnings multiples over the last 20 years (see Chart 10-1). The proverbial rising tide lifted all boats. It was also a huge boon for the growth in indexed funds, for it set the stage for relatively consistent double-digit returns over the same period.

But while there is little question that the Fed's victory in its historic struggle against inflation is good news, the bad news is that interest rates are now so low that equity investors have little to look forward to in terms of multiple expansion over the next several years. At least without a significant structural change in the economy like the recent cuts in the tax rates of capital gains and dividends. In the current environment, equity investors will be hard pressed to achieve returns significantly greater than whatever the growth in earnings turns out to be—historically about 7 percent annually.

But in much the same way that the long-term drop in interest rates from the early 1980s to 2003 was a justification for passive investing,

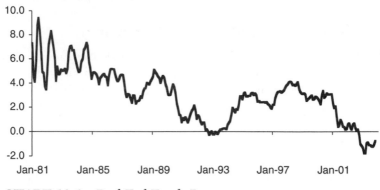

CHART 10-1   Real Fed Funds Rate

the low and moderate returns of the next decade suggest that salad days are ahead for good active managers.

As Chart 10-2 indicates, active management has a distinct advantage over passive management in periods of low and stable returns. According to data provided by Jeremy Siegel of the Wharton School, nearly 50 percent of general equity funds were able to beat the index when returns were below average, but only 26 percent were able to beat the index when returns were above average.

How can this be when the professional portfolio manager's only mission in life is to beat the benchmark?

Although at least part of this phenomenon can be attributed to the size of the asset management industry today (how many managers ultimately can be above average?), a more plausible explanation is that outsized returns are usually accompanied by valuations few professional money managers would find appealing, and big declines are accompanied by massive redemptions that wind up hurting returns. But there are other reasons as well.

First, almost all fund managers find it prudent to keep some cash position in their portfolios to meet redemptions. Second, most managers are broadly diversified, making their portfolios more closely resemble an equal-weighted index than a market-cap weighted one like the S&P 500. And both the tendency to hold cash and be diversified hurts the relative performance of active managers in hot markets when highly priced large cap stocks tend to get larger and more expensive.

Perhaps one of the best examples of this phenomenon occurred in the late 1990s. Indeed, with average total returns on the S&P of 26.3

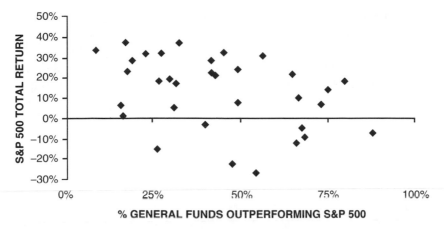

CHART 10-2   Active Management Performance and Total Return

percent from 1995 to 1999, all but the most risk-loving investors found it difficult to beat their benchmarks. Similarly, the massive declines in stock prices once the bubble had burst made it difficult for the fully invested professional manager to do anything but underperform. Aside from raising large amounts of cash, there were simply too many companies carried out on a stretcher for the average active manager to avoid them. Though the economy's structural problems are far from resolved and anxieties about terrorism and national security persist, the good news is that it is difficult to imagine a more dramatic market environment than the one experienced in the aftermath of the peak in stocks in 2000.

Active managers should benefit from the fact that higher interest rates will likely lead to far more moderate returns over the next several years than were seen in the late 1990s, and hopefully to more stable returns than those experienced from 2000 to 2002.

Low Nominal Growth

Perhaps the strongest argument for active management rests with the fact that index investing unnecessarily exposes investors to performance-crushing returns on stocks of marginal companies. While this is always the case, the chances of survival for weak companies are far less certain in an environment where debt levels are high and interest rates are more likely to rise than to fall. As we saw in Chapter 5, the emergence of truly global markets is intensifying the competitive nature of free market capitalism and exacerbating the difference between winners and losers across all industries. Providing fertile ground for winner-take-all markets, tighter monetary policies and the potential for lower than average nominal growth may make it difficult for marginal players to survive. This brave new world has major implications for how portfolios should be constructed, and it gives active managers a decided edge over their passive competition.

This is because, in more challenging economic environments, outperformance ultimately becomes a function of avoiding the worst stocks rather than owning the best ones. Typically, owning the bottom performing decile in the S&P 500 hurts. But in periods of below average nominal growth, owning the worst performing stocks has ended the careers of many a sell-side strategist and portfolio manager alike. A former chief investment strategist at Morgan Stanley, Steve Galbraith, put it this way in an interview with *Institutional Investor* magazine in 2002:

> **Blowups are costing more. Owning the 20 worst performing stocks in the S&P has historically cost investors around 110 basis points, but more recently, the cost has been close to 300 basis points. In a business where over time a few hundred basis points separates the megastars from the has-beens, playing defense should be of more than academic interest to fund managers and clients.[4]**

In more difficult investment environments, active managers should have a clear edge in avoiding this bottom decile. In many ways it seems that 2003 may have been the big WOW finish to the passive management tsunami that started in 1981. Indeed, one of the curious features of the market's performance in 2003 is that companies without earnings outperformed those with earnings. It seems hard to believe, but again, the punch line can be found in interest rates that were so low that even the most financially troubled could survive. Despite this fact, active managers had a decent year, with nearly 41 percent beating the S&P 500. When both short- and long-term interest rates begin to rise again, it's likely that active managers will do even better.

The Size of Indexed Assets

One of the central ironies about passive investing is that the public's desire to index increases in periods of maximum risk and decreases in periods of maximum opportunity. In the first six months of 1999, for example, nearly 70 percent of the money invested was placed in indexed funds. Although it may seem a minor point, active managers may also have an edge over their passive competition simply because of the way in which the indices themselves are constructed.

Indexed assets have grown from $100 billion in the early 1990s to almost $1 trillion today. As Jeremy Siegel has pointed out, this hyper-growth in passive investing often forces companies to enter benchmarks at inflated prices, lowering future potential returns. As an example, Yahoo! went up 64 percent between the day its entry into the S&P was announced and the day it actually went into the index. The S&P itself found that shares entering the 500 rose 8.5 percent on average between the time their admission into the S&P was announced and the effective date of their entry.[5] Siegel has postulated that lower bid-ask spreads might offset the impact of this premium but would probably not be enough to completely offset it.

Perhaps the greatest evidence of this phenomenon came from a working paper in December 2001 from the esteemed National Bureau of Economic Research, the organization charged with offi-cially putting start and end dates on recessions and recoveries. Using Tobin's q ratio, a popular academic measure of valuation put forth by Nobel Prize–winning economist James Tobin,[6] the authors of the paper, Randall Morck and Fan Yang, found that stocks included in the S&P 500 did indeed trade at a premium to similar companies that were not. Further, they found that this premium has grown with the advent of indexation.

In 1978 the difference between the average q ratio for companies in the S&P and similar companies outside the index was negligible. By 1997, however, companies within the S&P had a mean q ratio of 2.3, while those outside the index were far cheaper, with a mean ratio of 1.8.[7] The authors concluded that indexing might be:

> ... **undermining the efficiency of the stock market. In an "index-ing bubble," index stock prices spiral upward due to rising demand from index funds due to the superior past performance of indexing, which is due to the upward spiral of index stock prices. ... This second interpretation of our findings is consis-tent with the view that such an indexing bubble occurred in the U.S. stock market."**[8]

The bottom line is that as the public's love affair with indexation grows, the public itself will be buying stocks at higher and less justified prices. This necessarily limits the potential returns for passive investors.

The Declining Usefulness of the S&P 500

Even if an investor can slough off the arguments about what will likely be a far less appealing environment for indexation, there is a growing concern that the standard index for passive investing, the S&P 500, is an inappropriate benchmark.

Many academics have argued that the 500 only represents about 80 percent of the total capitalization of U.S. stocks. Other critics have noted that Standard & Poor's frequent additions and deletions to the index is a form of active management itself, and that its market-cap weighting produces a precarious level of concentration. At the start of 2004, for instance, the top 25 stocks in the S&P 500 comprised nearly 37 percent of the index—clearly antithetical to the idea of diversification most investors look for when choosing a passively managed fund. As a result, an increasing number of investors are choosing the more broadly diversified Wilshire 5000 and Russell 3000 as true proxies for the broader market.

Mutual Funds Still Make Sense

For many individual investors, the mutual fund scandals involving market timing and late trading were the final sad and ignominious piece of evidence that those entrusted to act as their fiduciaries—corporate chieftains, brokers, and portfolio managers—had failed them. It may not be politically correct to say this, but for all of the hype in the press and the wringing of hands and gnashing of teeth that these scandals engendered, a simple yet crucial message about mutual funds was lost in translation in the last few years: No financial structure in history has helped so many people build wealth as did the simple, standard mutual fund.

Index fund complexes and their new cousin, exchange-traded funds—or ETFs—have all done their best to take advantage of this latest chapter in the corporate malfeasance saga. But as we have seen in this chapter, not enough has been written in the popular media about the potential pitfalls of index investing or the advantages of investing in actively managed mutual funds.

Despite all the recent bad press, mutual funds are a cost-effective way to gain broad diversification and low tracking errors. Most actively managed equity funds provide their services for less than 1 percent of assets under management and, for as little as $1,000 in some cases— to get started—offer investors literally hundreds of stocks.

Although there is quite a bit of academic research to suggest that diversification can be achieved with as few as 15 to 20 stocks, investors leave themselves open to higher tracking errors when they decide to go it alone. In the winter 2000 *Journal of Investing*, Ronald Surz and Mitchell Price calculated that investors should expect a tracking error of 5.4 percentage points a year in a 15-stock portfolio. That means that in any given year in which the market returns 10 percent, investors could expect returns of 4.6 or 15.4 percent. The only way to truly eliminate that risk is to own hundreds of stocks, which is the greatest advantage mutual funds have to offer.[9]

In recent years exchange-traded funds, or ETFs, have been touted as the lowest-cost and most tax-effective way to gain exposure to a wide variety of stocks. Certainly, few financial products have grown so quickly. Assets in ETFs have grown from virtually zero five years ago to more than $155 billion in July 2003.[10]

To be sure, ETFs offer a number of advantages over traditional mutual funds: They can be bought and sold throughout the day and are therefore more liquid, they have lower expense ratios (typically between 0.1 and 0.65 percent), and they only create taxable events when the shares are bought and sold. But largely absent from the discussion of ETFs has been their greatest weakness for investors seeking to dollar-cost-average by making regular systematic investments in stocks and bonds: brokerage commissions and the presence of a bid-ask spread.[11] These costs make the fairly standard $50 or $100 a month investment prohibitively more expensive than what can be achieved in traditional mutual fund investments.

Of course, because of their higher fees and a potentially more onerous capital gains profile, actively managed mutual funds won't always be the right answer for those seeking to maximize returns. But for the reasons stated earlier in this chapter—the greater potential for stable and lower average total returns, a lower nominal growth environment, and the sheer size of assets in indexed funds—the next few years might well produce excess returns for those who invest in actively managed mutual funds.

Thoughts on the Recent Scandals

The last few years have been tough on investors of mutual funds. But while there is little doubt that instances of late trading—where select customers were able to buy mutual funds after the close at the closing price—were harmful to other investors and clearly illegal, the jury is still out on how much the far more common practice of market timing—where certain investors were allowed to trade in and out funds in rapid fashion—actually hurt the average investor.

Some have suggested that, at most, market timing may have cost investors $10, or 1 percent, for every $1,000 investment in mutual funds. Others have suggested that the impact of market timing had, net-net, absolutely no impact on long-term investors. This is not to say that these practices are not potentially harmful to investors who play by the rules. There are few serious professionals on Wall Street who would argue that instances of late trading should not be prosecuted fully or that the practice of market timing shouldn't be significantly curtailed or stopped altogether. But unfortunately, not enough people in my business stood in the docket and defended our industry against the implied assertion in the media and from the New York State Attorney General that the brokerage and mutual fund industries routinely put their own interests above those of their clients.

There are, of course, bad actors in all businesses. But spending almost three months a year on the road visiting this country's top money managers year in and year out, I feel strongly that the vast majority of portfolio managers are doing their best to act as fiduciaries for their clients. A good friend of mine, a prominent mutual fund manager, put it to me this way:

> **Jason, we currently have 600 portfolio managers in our system worldwide and another 300 to 400 that now work at other firms. If only one these people acted improperly, even if it was three years ago, the current ethos in the media makes it very easy to impugn the reputation of our entire firm. It's simply not fair. Unfortunately, the regulatory environment in our industry is now so strict that few people have the courage to stand up for themselves, lest they be the next target for an overeager prosecutor.**

Some of the mutual fund industry's harshest critics have suggested that regulators should actually set the mutual fund industry's fee structure. While it seems reasonable that regulators and states' attorneys general should seek reforms from companies it has found to be in violation of securities laws, it seems odd to me that they should be in the business of dictating the prices of any business. It would be roughly akin to the Department of Health, after discovering substandard levels of cleanliness in the kitchen of a local restaurant, dictating what it might be able to charge for a hamburger.

In fact, many professionals on Wall Street believe that greater regulatory scrutiny of our industry will make it stronger in the long run. But they have legitimate concerns about whether the economy as a whole would function more efficiently if regulators and prosecutors, rather than the invisible hand of free markets, should engage in the practice of setting prices.

In an environment where the investment industry is doing its best to reform and where regulators use their power judiciously, few doubt that mutual funds and active managers could enjoy a bright future. Given the challenges inherent in today's global economy and financial markets, the Lord only knows that not all money managers will be able to survive on today's new Wall Street. But the challenges of our current low nominal environment, the inherent weaknesses of index investing, and the prospects for more moderate and stable returns should all benefit skilled managers over their passive investment competition in the decade to come.

Key Take-Aways

1. Already low interest rates will make multiple expansion difficult to achieve over the next decade. Low and stable return environments have historically favored active managers over their passive competition.
2. Higher interest rates and greater global competition are exacerbating the differences between winners and losers in the economy and in the stock market. As a result, investment mistakes are becoming far more costly. Active managers should have a decided edge in avoiding performance-crushing stocks in equity portfolios.
3. The size of the indexed fund market forces companies into the index at inflated prices, limiting future potential returns.
4. More broadly diversified indices like the Wilshire 5000 and the Russell 3000 may be more appropriate proxies for broad equity market returns than the S&P 500.
5. Despite the headlines, mutual funds are still a cost-effective way to gain broad diversification and low tracking errors in stock portfolios.

CONCLUSION

THE WHOLE POINT OF *New Markets, New Strategies* is that investing is not as difficult as it appeared in the early part of this decade, nor is it as easy as it appeared in the latter part of the last one.

If there were a lesson to be derived from our most recent experience with a bear market it was that investors should behave not as gamblers, but as lenders of capital. In this regard, a renewed focus on tried and true investment techniques along with recognition of how Wall Street has changed should be a powerful combination in the decade to come.

Dividends and corporate governance will be increasingly important themes, and the names of Wall Street's major players will change. Regulators are likely to cast a longer shadow, hedge funds rather than mutual funds will become the big marginal buyers and sellers of stocks, and the best research will likely be done far from the canyons of Wall Street.

More global competition and greater government regulation will mean that only the best companies will prosper, favoring aggressive and tenacious companies that seek to dominate their markets. It will also present greater challenges for the intelligent investor, requiring increased vigilance and hard work.

In the last few years the word "optimist" has taken on a negative connotation on Wall Street, in the media, and in society. The bear market has made it easy to view people who are pessimistic and skeptical as more serious and at times more intelligent than those who like to look at the glass as half full. The voices of those who claim that America can't compete because its labor costs are too high or its population too old or its educational system too weak have sounded loudest in the last few years. But it's important to remember that the vast swath of history favors the optimist.

Economic progress and investment success won't be easily attained in the decade to come. They rarely are. America can only maintain its economic might if it embraces the concepts of free trade and technology, which have been at the heart of its economy for the last two centuries. And investors will only be successful if they believe in themselves.

To quote Ronald Reagan: "I, too, have been described as an undying optimist, always seeing a glass half full when some see it as half empty. And, yes, it's true—I always see the sunny side of life. . . . My optimism comes not just from my strong faith in God, but from my strong and enduring faith in man."

Jason Trennert
New York, New York

NOTES

Part I

Chapter 1

1. Jeremy Siegel. *Stocks for the Long Run.* New York: McGraw Hill, 1994, 71.
2. Richard A. Brealey and Stewart C. Meyers. *Principles of Corporate Finance,* 4th edition. New York: McGraw-Hill, 383.
3. "Microsoft Has the Cash, and Holders Suggest a Dividend," *Wall Street Journal,* January 2, 2002.
4. Robert D. Arnott and Clifford S. Asness, "Surprise! Higher Dividends = Higher Earnings Growth," *Financial Analysts Journal,* January-February 2003, 70–87.
5. "Republicans Relent on Tax Cuts to Get Budget Deal," *Wall Street Journal,* April 14, 2003.
6. "Nurturing the Tax Cut Idea Since the Era of Reagan," *New York Times,* June 6, 2003.
7. Tim Gray, "Investing: Here Come the Dividends. But Don't Cheer Yet," *New York Times,* September 14, 2003.
8. Philip Brown and Alex Clarke, "The Ex-Dividend Day Behavior of Australian Share Prices Before and After Dividend Imputation," working paper, University of New South Wales, 1993.

Chapter 2

1. Francois-Serge Lhabitant. *Hedge Funds.* Sussex, England, John Wiley, 2002, 27–28.
2. Ibid, 7.
3. John Brooks. *The Go-Go Years.* New York: John Wiley, 1999, 142.
4. Lhabitant, 8.
5. Ibid.

6. James J. Cramer. *Confessions of a Street Addict*. New York: Simon & Schuster, 2002, 53.
7. Erin Arvedlund, "Market Wizards," *Barron's*, October 6, 2003, L3.

Chapter 3

1. Ron Insana. *The Message of the Markets*. New York: Harper Business, 2000, 134–140.
2. *2002 Annual Report*, L-3 Communications (NYSE: LLL).
3. Sebastian Moffett and Martin Fackler, "Cautiously, Japan Returns to Combat, in Southern Iraq," *Wall Street Journal*, January 2, 2004.
4. My right-hand man, Nicholas Bohnsack of ISI, greatly aided in the research for this section of the chapter.
5. John Dennis Brown. *101 Years on Wall Street*. Englewood Cliffs, New Jersey: Prentice Hall, 1991, 203–204.
6. Wallace Carroll, "Steel: A 72-Hour Drama with an All-Star Cast," *New York Times*, April 22, 1962.
7. "Trial Lawyers Inc." New York: Manhattan Institute, 2003.
8. Ibid., 20.

Chapter 4

1. Edwin Lefevre. *Reminiscences of a Stock Operator*. Burlington, Vermont: Traders Press, 1980, 10.
2. John Mickelthwait and Adrian Wooldridge. *The Company*. New York: The Modern Library, 2003, 73.
3. John Kenneth Galbraith. *A Short History of Financial Euphoria*. New York: Penguin Publishing, 1993, 22.
4. Michael Lewis. *The Money Culture*. New York: W.W. Norton, 1991, 98.
5. James J. Smalhout, "Doing Well by Doing Good," *Barron's Online*, January 27, 2003. *Barron's Dictionary of Finance and Investment Terms* defines a "poison pill" as "a strategic move by a takeover-target company to make its stock less attractive to an acquirer. For instance, a firm may issue a new series of Preferred Stock that gives shareholders the right to redeem it at a premium price after a takeover." It defines a "golden parachute" as a "lucrative contract given to a top executive to provide lavish benefits in case the company is taken over by another firm, resulting in the loss of the job."
6. Roger Lowenstein, "The Company They Kept.," *New York Times Magazine*, February 1, 2004, 28.
7. Mickeltwait and Wooldridge, 136.
8. Galbraith, 109.
9. Robert A.G. Monks and Nell Minow. *Corporate Governance*, 2nd edition. Malden, Massachusetts: Blackwell Publishers, 2001, 164–166.
10. Ibid., 172.
11. Ibid., 210.
12. Mickelthwait and Wooldridge. 136.

13. James Smalhout, "Doing Well by Doing Good." *Barron's Online*, January 27, 2003.
14. Monks and Minow, 195.
15. Mickelthwait and Wooldridge, 141.
16. Amy Borrus, "Board, Interrupted," *BusinessWeek*, October 13, 2003, 114–115.
17. Monks and Minow, 47.
18. Paul Gompers, Joy Ishii, and Andrew Metrick, "Corporate Governance and Equity Prices," *The Quarterly Journal of Economics*, February 2003, 107–155.

Chapter 5

1. John Mickelthwait and Adrian Wooldridge. *The Company.* New York: The Modern Library, 2003, 173.
2. Ibid., 129.
3. Ibid., 179.
4. "China: Awakening Giant," Federal Reserve Bank of Dallas, Southwest Economy, September/October 2003, 2–7.
5. "The Hungry Dragon," *The Economist,* February 21, 2004, 59–60.
6. "China: Awakening Giant," Federal Reserve Bank of Dallas, 3.
7. Bureau of Labor Statistics.
8. "China: Awakening Giant," Federal Reserve Bank of Dallas, 3.
9. Dominick Salvatore. *International Economics,* 2nd edition. New York: Macmillan, 1987, 16.
10. Thomas Friedman, *New York Times,* February 26, 2004, op-ed page.
11. Walter Wriston, "Ever Heard of Insourcing?" *Wall Street Journal,* March 24, 2004, A20.
12. James C. Cooper, "The Price of Efficiency," *BusinessWeek,* March 22, 2004, 41.
13. Brian Wesbury. *The New Era of Wealth.* New York: McGraw-Hill, 2000, 20.
14. Mickelthwait, 131.
15. Bruce Nussbaum, "Where Are the Jobs?" *BusinessWeek*, March 22, 2004, 37.
16. Joseph Schumpeter. *Capitalism, Socialism, and Democracy.* New York: Harper & Row, 1942, 83.
17. Mickelthwait, 129.

Part II

Chapter 6

1. Fred Schwed, Jr. *Where Are the Customers Yachts?* New York: John Wiley & Sons, Inc., 1995, 37.
2. Donald Weeden. *Weeden & Company.* New York: Donald E. Weeden, 2002.
3. Russell O.Wright. *Chronology of the Stock Market.* Jefferson, North Carolina: McFarland & Company, 1981.

4. Ibid.

5. "25 Years: The Heroes, Villains, Triumphs, Failures and Other Memorable Events," *Institutional Investor,* July 1992.

6. Chris Welles. *The Last Days of the Club.* New York: E.P. Dutton & Co., 1975, 69.

7. Alex Berenson. *The Number.* New York: Random House, 2003, 88.

8. Ron Insana. *Traders' Tales.* New York, John Wiley, 1996.

9. Faith Keenan, "Bad Advice," *Bloomberg Magazine*, July 2000.

10. Ibid.

11. Jonah Keri, "Analysts Make Stock Calls, but Market Doesn't Listen," *Investor's Business Daily,* September 15, 2003

12. John Vail, "When Sell-Side Research Was Made Illegal," Mizuho Securities, July 26, 2002.

13. Ibid.

14. Jesse Eisinger, "Ahead of the Tape: The Veil Drops,"*Wall Street Journal,*October 9, 2003.

15. StarMine promotional material, November 2003.

Chapter 7

1. Kenneth L. Fischer. *100 Minds That Made the Market.* Woodside, California: Business Classics, 1993, 301.

2. David Dreman. *Contrarian Investment Strategies: The Next Generation.* New York: Simon & Schuster, 1998, 377.

3. Lawrence Minard, "The Original Contrarian," *Forbes*, September 26, 1983, 42–52.

4. Ibid.

5. Minard, 43.

6. Fischer, 313.

7. John Maynard Keynes. *General Theory of Employment, Interest, and Money,* Amherst, NY: Prometheus Books, reprinted 1997 (originally published 1935), 154.

8. Ibid.

9. Minard, 43.

10. Minard, 52.

11. Fischer, 312–315.

12. Ibid.

13. Investor's Business Daily. *Guide to High-Performance Investing.* Los Angeles: O'Neil Data Systems, 1993, 30.

14. Erin Arvedlund, "Market Wizards," *Barron's*, October 6, 2003, L3.

15. Take a guess as to where the majority of Harvard grads want to go now. That's right: hedge funds.

16. Gustave LeBon. *The Crowd: A Study of the Popular Mind.* London: T. Fisher Unwin, reprinted 2003 (originally published 1896), 32–33.

Chapter 8

1. Aswath Damodoran. *Investment Valuation*. New York: John Wiley, 1996, 2.
2. Peter Lynch. *One Up on Wall Street*. New York: Penguin Books, 1990, 155–56.
3. Ibid., 165.
4. Jeremy Siegel. *Stocks for the Long Run*. New York: McGraw-Hill, 2002, 99.
5. *BusinessWeek* highlighted this development in an August 9, 1958, article entitled "An Evil Omen Returns," 81.
6. These figures were based on those available in June 2004.

Chapter 9

1. The difference between long and short-term interest rates.

Chapter 10

1. Rich Blake, "Is Time Running Out for the S&P 500?" *Institutional Investor*, May 2002, 58.
2. Charles Ellis, "The Loser's Game." In *An Investor's Anthology*. New York: John Wiley, 2002, 167.
3. Blake, 59.
4. Ibid., 58.
5. Jeremy Siegel. *Stocks for the Long Run*. New York: McGraw-Hill, 2002.
6. Tobin's q is the ratio of the value of a firm's assets and their replacement value.
7. Randall Morck and Fan Yang. *The Mysterious Growing Value of S&P 500 Membership*. Cambridge, Massachusetts: National Bureau of Economic Research, December 2001, 36.
8. Ibid., 32.
9. Jonathan Clements, "Despite Scandals, Funds Still Offer Advantages Over Any Other Investment," *Wall Street Journal*, December 2003.
10. Yahoo Finance, ETF Center: Frequently Asked Questions, www.ETFZone.com, 2004.
11. The bid-ask spread is the difference between the price at which shares can be purchased (the asking price) and the price at which shares can be sold (the bid price).

INDEX

Index

About the Author

Jason Trennert is Chief Investment Strategiest and Senior Managing Director at International Strategy and Investment Group Inc. (ISI Group), a New York broker-dealer specializing in economic research. He is head of ISI's investment strategy team, ranked runners-up in the *Institutional Investor* 2003 All America Research Team and Best Boutique for Portfolio Strategy. He is regularly quoted in the domestic and foreign press, is a regular guest host on CNBC's *Squawk Box,* and has been a special guest on *Kudlow & Cramer* and *Louis Rukeyser's Wall Street.*